Pinata Economics

Lucas Brooks

Published by Kokosnuss Press, 2025.

PINATA ECONOMICS

First edition. September 4, 2025.

ISBN: 979-8232119133

Written by Lucas Brooks.

Table of Contents

Introduction: "Grab the Stick"

The piñata hangs from the ceiling: bright, festive, seemingly innocent. Kids gather beneath it with blindfolds on, giggling, waiting for the candy to fall. Someone hands a child the stick. They swing. The candy scatters — or, more realistically, a small handful drops while the rest stays stubbornly inside. Someone else gets another turn. Meanwhile, a few kids near the ladder — the ones with the clearest view — have secret pockets and a plan. They collect what falls. Some of them quietly pull the ropes that make the piñata harder to break. The party continues, the music plays, and the adults say, "It's fine — the candy will trickle down."

That is the image at the heart of this book. It's charming until you notice who is actually getting the candy, who is kept away from the stick, and how the piñata itself has been reinforced. Pinata Economics is not an argument against parties. It is an argument about fairness, about power, and about the decisions that shape how resources are distributed in a society. It asks a simple question: if the goal is a genuinely flourishing community — healthier people, safer neighborhoods, thriving schools and workplaces — what do we need to do differently? The blunt answer is: grab the stick, aim the swing, and change the way the piñata is made.

The Piñata as a Metaphor — Why it Fits

Simple metaphors are valuable because they help us see complex systems. The piñata is especially useful because it packages several truths into a single, memorable image.

First, the piñata contains something desirable — candy, treats, resources. In economic terms, these are goods and services that make life worth living: health care, housing, education, clean air, meaningful work, and the resources necessary for people to pursue their ambitions.

Second, access to those goods depends on rules and structures. Who gets to swing, who picks up what falls, who has the ladder — these are institutional questions. In the economy, these correspond to tax codes, property regimes, labor laws, corporate governance, education funding, and political rules.

Third, the distribution of what's inside the piñata is not accidental. The piñata can be hollow, fortified, or opened by design. Likewise, economic arrangements are designed — sometimes intentionally to concentrate wealth, sometimes unintentionally through inertia. The image helps us evade a popular fatalism: the idea that whatever falls must have been "deserved."

Fourth, the more you look, the more you see hidden mechanisms: hidden pockets, ropes, who controls the ladder, and who sets the rules of the game. In real life, those hidden mechanisms are tax loopholes, lobbying, unequal bargaining power, discriminatory zoning, and private wealth that buys political influence.

The piñata helps us see that distribution is about power. It is a moral argument dressed as an economic argument: we accept some rules because they're convenient for those in power, not because they are fair or socially optimal. If we are honest, we must face another truth the metaphor makes plain: if the party is to be fair, someone has to take hold of the stick and swing.

The Central Claim: Trickle-Down Is a Golden Lie

"Trickle-down" is the shorthand for a set of ideas: that giving resources to the wealthy spurs investment, which spreads benefits to everyone; that lowering taxes on capital and the rich will revive entrepreneurship and job creation; that markets allocate rewards to the most deserving, and so the wealthy are simply earning what they deserve. These ideas are not innocent errors. They are political narratives with deep rhetorical power: they promise both efficiency and moral clarity. Who would argue against growth and rewards for merit?

But the trickle-down story rests on shaky assumptions. It assumes that wealth necessarily converts into broad-based investment and job creation, that markets are free of powerful distortions, and that political systems are neutral arbiters rather than instruments of influence. In practice, concentrated wealth often does not trickle — it pools, it shelters, it buys influence, and it compounds. The "golden" part of the lie is the halo around success: we celebrate those at the top as innovators and creators, while overlooking how rules and networks often prop them up.

Accepting trickle-down has practical effects. It shapes policy — tax cuts for the wealthy, deregulation, weakening of unions, and neglect of public investment. It channels public attention away from structural change and toward individual effort. It justifies a passive hope that growth will suffice: give the piñata to the few and believe that the candy will eventually find its way down.

But what if it doesn't? What if, instead of generosity, the wealthy use their gains to fortify the piñata? What if the rules are written to keep candy in the pockets of the few? The evidence — across different countries and eras — suggests that when power becomes concentrated, outcomes reflect power, not merit. Trickle-down is a political argument deployed to keep structures in place; it is not a neutral economic law.

To transform outcomes, we must move from passive belief to active design. The problem is not scarcity — societies have produced extraordinary wealth. The problem is its distribution and the rules that determine it. That is the book's central claim: redistribution must be an active process, not a passive waiting game.

Why This Is Urgent Now

Arguments about fairness are perennial. What makes this moment acute are three overlapping crises that expose and intensify inequality: the global pandemic, the climate emergency, and the extraordinary concentration of private wealth and power.

1. The pandemic made inequality visible — and lethal. COVID-19 did more than pause economies; it exposed the fragility of a system in which basic security depends on contingent employment, precarious savings, and the benevolence of employers. Those with steady incomes, savings, or generous health benefits could shelter in place. Many low-wage workers — grocery clerks, delivery drivers, home care workers — faced exposure on the job. The pandemic also revealed how public health and economic well-being are intertwined: countries with stronger public health systems and social safety nets were better able to cushion the blow. The lesson is stark: when risks are systemic, private arrangements fail to protect the many.

2. Climate change multiplies vulnerability and concentrates costs. The climate crisis is not an abstract future; it is redistributive in the present. Heatwaves, floods, fires, and storms hit hardest where infrastructure is weakest and insurance is scarce. Poorer communities — often marginalized by historical policies like redlining and inadequate public investment — bear the brunt. Meanwhile, those with wealth can retreat to safer locations, build private defenses, or purchase insurance. If our goal is resilience and justice, we must channel resources deliberately to protect the many rather than the few.

3. Wealth concentration has reached historic levels of power and influence. Across advanced economies and many developing ones, private wealth has grown faster than incomes and public investment. The wealthy can shelter assets in complex financial instruments, buy political influence through lobbying and campaign donations, and shape narratives through media ownership. This concentration changes the rules of the game. When wealth shapes law and policy, the notion of a fair contest collapses. The piñata is not just a toy — it becomes a fortress.

These crises interact. A pandemic disproportionately harms those already vulnerable because political choices left them exposed. Climate shocks compound economic precarity. Wealthy actors can influence response policies to their advantage—shaping bailouts, tax relief, procurement contracts, and regulatory rollbacks. The combination is not merely an academic worry; it is a recipe for entrenched inequality and a degraded democratic commons.

This is why the argument for active redistribution is not optional or ideological — it is practical. It is about protecting the conditions under which people can live decently and participate in civic life. It is about resilience and shared security, not punishment.

Redistribution Must Be Active — The Logic

There are two basic ways to think about redistribution. The first is passive: hope that market outcomes, perhaps nudged by a few incentives, will balance out. The second is active: design institutions and policies to distribute resources deliberately, with clear goals and mechanisms.

Passive redistribution assumes a generous faith in self-correcting markets. It imagines that if the wealthy are allowed to accumulate, their investments will automatically create jobs and prosperity for all. Active redistribution assumes something different: that markets operate within rules, that those rules can be changed, and that fairness requires intervention. Active redistribution is, in short, governance. It uses law, public spending, regulation, and social institutions to shape outcomes.

Why is active redistribution necessary? Because when power is concentrated, markets do not self-correct toward broad welfare. Markets are embedded in political and social institutions; they are not autonomous forces. Wealth buys influence over those institutions. Even well-intentioned market incentives are often gamed, producing outcomes that benefit those with the most resources. Without deliberate intervention, the system tends toward greater concentration.

Active redistribution is not about envy or punitive expropriation. It is about creating rules and institutions that make progress possible for everyone: functioning health systems, public education, infrastructure, an economy where people can form unions, access to capital for small businesses, and fair taxation so the public can invest in common goods. It recognizes that inequality is not merely an unfortunate side effect of progress — it is a political choice reflected in the rules we accept.

Active redistribution also recognizes the moral case: societies with lower inequality tend to enjoy better health, higher social trust, and stronger democratic institutions. In short, redistribution is both instrumentally smart and ethically defensible.

Introducing the Stick — Tools of Redistribution

If redistribution must be active, what are the tools — the sticks — by which we can break the piñata? The metaphor is useful because a stick is straightforward: it's an implement that lets someone open what's inside. But the choice of stick matters. A weak twig won't do. A hammer in the wrong hands can be destructive. The point is not brute force; it is effective, skillful action that opens the piñata and distributes the candy widely and fairly.

Below are the categories of tools we will examine in this book. Each is a way of steering resources toward broader public benefit. Each has trade-offs, political impediments, and technical design questions. We will confront those honestly in later chapters. For now, think of these as the basic implements in a toolbox.

1. Progressive taxation and public investment. Taxes are the most direct mechanism to move resources from concentrated private wealth to public goods. Progressive taxation — where those with greater ability to pay contribute more — supports investments in health, education, housing, and infrastructure. Public investment creates shared capacity: roads, schools, research, and social insurance that enable people to pursue productive lives.

But taxation is not just about collection. It's also about design: how to tax income, capital, inheritance, and wealth; how to close loopholes; and how to enforce rules across borders. Tax policy shapes incentives and what is politically possible. We will examine realistic tax reforms and how to defend them.

2. Labor power: unions and collective bargaining. Wages and working conditions don't float freely; they are the result of bargaining power. Unions have historically been one of the most effective sticks for redistributing income, because collective bargaining changes who sets the terms in workplaces. When workers can bargain, wages and benefits rise, and inequality narrows.

Revitalizing labor requires both legal change and organizing strategies. It also requires new models for the gig economy and precarious work. Strengthening workers' rights is not a backward step; it's an update to make sure labor markets are fair in a changing economy.

3. Antitrust and corporate governance. Concentration of corporate power reduces competition, weakens worker bargaining, and allows firms to extract rents. Antitrust enforcement and corporate governance reforms can break up excessive market power, restore competitive dynamics, and reorient companies toward broader stakeholder responsibilities.

This is not merely about breaking big firms for the sake of size; it's about ensuring markets serve citizens, not the consolidation of influence.

4. Public ownership, co-ops, and democratized capital. In areas where markets fail to deliver equitable outcomes — utilities, crucial infrastructure, housing — public ownership and cooperative forms can provide services without extracting excessive profit. Democratizing capital — through community wealth funds, public banks, municipal ownership, and worker co-ops — keeps value circulating locally and equitably.

The choice between public, private, and cooperative ownership is contextual. Each has strengths and governance requirements. The key is design that aligns provision with public good.

5. Social guarantees and transfers. Programs like universal health care, child allowances, unemployment insurance, and even explorations of universal basic income are ways to provide baseline security. Transfers reduce poverty, stabilize demand, and free people to take risks (start businesses, change jobs) without immediate destitution.

Design matters: means-testing versus universality, conditionality, and how programs integrate with labor markets and caregiving responsibilities. A core point is that social guarantees are investments in human capital and civic stability.

6. Anti-corruption and democratic reforms. Redistribution fails if the political system is captured. Campaign finance reform, transparency, limits on lobbying, and rules against revolving doors are necessary to prevent the wealthy from writing policies in their favor. Electoral reforms — from public financing of campaigns to better representation — protect the democratic space where redistribution is debated and decided.

7. International coordination. In a globalized economy, capital can cross borders. Tax havens, regulatory arbitrage, and unequal trade rules undermine national efforts. International cooperation on tax enforcement, corporate transparency, and climate financing is essential. National policies alone cannot fully address the mobility of capital; coordinated global action can level the playing field.

8. Narrative and cultural strategies. Policies succeed or fail not only on mechanics but on stories. The myth of meritocracy and the rhetoric of scarcity are powerful. Reframing public discourse — emphasizing shared fate, the value of care, and the public benefits of investment — is a stick of a different sort: the ability to shape consent and mobilize support.

These tools are not magic bullets. Each comes with limitations and political resistance. They can be combined in many ways. Some reforms might look symbolic but can be leverage points; others require long, patient institution-building. The essential insight is that there is a toolbox — and the composition and sequence of tools determine outcomes.

What This Book Is — And What It Isn't

It is tempting to imagine that a single chapter could map every policy and political strategy. This book does not pretend to be a complete, technical manual for every jurisdiction. Instead, it aims to do three things well.

First, it provides a clear diagnosis. We will show how inequality is produced and sustained by laws, institutions, and the strategic behavior of powerful actors. Diagnosis matters because good policy begins with a correct understanding of the causal mechanisms at work.

Second, it offers a pragmatic framework for action. That means concrete policy options, historical examples, and strategy for organizing and political change. We will weigh trade-offs honestly and offer sequencing and tactics that are politically viable—not merely idealistic.

Third, it presents a vision: why redistribution matters beyond numbers. This is about democratic health, personal dignity, and the kind of society we want to inhabit. Policies are not ends; they are means to a civilization that gives everyone a stake.

What this book is not: it is not a polemic for punitive redistribution or an academic treatise full of technicalities meant only for economists. It is not a promise that change will be easy. It does not assume unanimous agreement. But it does assume this: that people care about fairness, about community, and about enduring institutions that make progress possible for all.

Preview of the Journey — How the Book is Organized

If the first task is to grab the stick, the second is to learn how to swing it well. The rest of this book is organized to do precisely that.

We begin by tracing the ideas and institutions that have hardened the piñata: the history of trickle-down rhetoric, the mechanics of wealth hoarding, and the myth of meritocracy. Understanding how the piñata is fortified is the precondition for effective action.

Then we shift to tools: taxation, labor power, antitrust, public ownership, social guarantees, democratic reforms, and international coordination. For each, we provide both the conceptual rationale and practical examples of where these tools have worked or failed. We emphasize design, not dogma: incremental reforms, bold experiments, and hybrid models will all appear.

Politics matters, so we devote chapters to counterattacks and cultural work. The wealthy and powerful do not cede advantage willingly. Movements win when they combine policy expertise with organizing, narrative, and legal strategy.

Finally, we argue for a vision of flourishing that goes beyond equalizing income: a robust public realm, dignified work, resilient communities, and institutions that protect hard-won gains. The last chapter is a playbook for mobilization and institutional safeguards — how to build change that lasts.

A Few Preemptive Answers

Some readers will object before they finish this chapter. Let me anticipate a few predictable worries.

"Won't redistribution hurt growth?" Growth is not a unitary phenomenon. Some forms of redistribution can, in theory, reduce certain private investments; others can boost aggregate demand, human capital, and long-term productive capacity. Investing in health, education, and infrastructure can enhance growth by expanding the capabilities of the workforce and enabling innovation. The debate is not whether redistribution affects incentives — it does — but how to design policies that maximize shared prosperity.

"Is redistribution just punishment for success?" No. Redistribution recognizes that markets operate inside rules that can be changed to better reflect shared values. It is corrective, not punitive: it invests in public goods that benefit everyone, including business. It also restores balance where power has distorted outcomes. Success can be celebrated while ensuring that success does not translate into a political license to hoard resources undemocratically.

"Won't people just game new rules?" Some will. People adapt to incentives. That's why policy design and enforcement matter. Good redistribution is not naïve; it anticipates avoidance, closes loopholes, and coordinates across borders where necessary. The alternative — resigning ourselves to inequality because some will cheat — is a recipe for stagnation.

"Isn't this ideological?" All economic arrangements are ideological to some degree because they reflect choices. The question is which ideology produces better lives for the many. This book argues that policies grounded in shared security, democratic participation, and public investment produce more durable, humane societies.

A Call to Action — Why You Should Care

You might not think of yourself as a voter, organizer, or policy wonk. Maybe you are a parent, a nurse, a teacher, a small-business owner, a technician, an artist. The truth is that redistribution affects all of those roles. It shapes whether your child has a good school, whether your workplace is safe, whether your neighborhood has resilient infrastructure, and whether the economy rewards skills and effort fairly.

The stakes are not merely economic. They are civic. Democracies rely on a sense of shared fate and mutual obligation. When the rules are visibly rigged, trust erodes. When civic institutions serve a narrow slice of society, political instability follows. Redistributing resources and power is thus also a project of strengthening democracy.

This book is an invitation. It asks readers to imagine a different balance of power and to consider the practical steps by which society could move toward that balance. It is both analytical and practical: we will name problems and offer tools. We will be honest about difficulty and realistic about trade-offs. And we will insist that the central moral question is not wealth for its own sake but what kind of life and fellowship a society should offer its members.

Closing Swing — A Small Demonstration

For a moment, return to the party. Picture the child with the stick. Now imagine the ladder is available to everyone, supervised by a fair referee, and the piñata is filled by the community rather than a secretive few. The first swing opens the candy — but more importantly, the rules of the game have changed. Everyone gets a turn. The party becomes a shared event rather than a spectacle where some are excluded. That change in rules is what Pinata Economics aims to achieve.

Our task is to think like builders rather than spectators. We will study the architecture of distribution, test the tools that can alter it, and confront the political forces that resist change. We will aim not for abstract purity but for pragmatic design: policies and institutions that improve people's lives and can be built and defended.

So grab the stick. The piñata is strong, but it is not invulnerable. The rest of this book is a guide to choosing the right stick, learning how to swing, and sharing what falls out.

The Golden Lie: How Trickle-Down Was Sold

If you want to sell a risky economic idea, wrap it in a story people already want to believe. Trickle-down economics did exactly that. It promised a tidy moral logic: reward success, and the benefits will wash outward; let wealth concentrate at the top and the whole society will be lifted. The rhetoric was simple, elegant, and morally comforting: the rich invest; investing creates jobs; jobs lift everyone. It fit an image of the market as an invisible hand that rewards merit. Who would argue with generosity that also boosts growth?

That rhetorical brilliance—its simplicity and moral brightness—is part of the reason trickle-down persisted even as its empirical record grew thin. It is not merely a failed economic hypothesis. It is a political story that justified a set of policy choices—tax cuts for high incomes, deregulation, weakened labor institutions, and an ideology of hands-off government—that reshaped how income and wealth are distributed. This chapter tells that story: where the idea came from, how it was sold, what policies sprung from it (especially under Presidents Reagan and George W. Bush), and why the promised benefits largely failed to arrive for most people. Along the way we'll examine the evidence: profits soaring, wages stagnating, inequality widening—and the research that ties these outcomes back to policy choices.

The Origin Story: Supply-Side Dress with a Libertarian Ribbon

The phrase "trickle-down" is a slightly contemptuous nickname, but the intellectual current behind it—supply-side economics and a strong preference for low taxation on capital—predates the Reagan era. Economists and policymakers in the 1970s and 1980s argued that carefully targeted reductions in marginal tax rates on investment and high incomes would unleash a wave of productive activity. The Laffer Curve—popularized by economist Art Laffer—offered a neat visual: cut taxes enough and you might increase economic activity so much that total revenue could stay constant or even rise.

Politically, supply-side economics married well with an older American strain of thought: free enterprise, small-government rhetoric, and the moral prestige of entrepreneurial success. Leading conservative intellectuals, think tanks, and sympathetic members of Congress pitched tax cuts as both efficiency-enhancing and morally right: citizens should keep the fruits of their labor, and less government interference would mean freer, richer markets. Reagan—a charismatic carrier of these themes—made the logic central to his 1980 campaign and presidency, promising tax relief as a route out of stagflation and economic malaise.

That political fusion transformed ideas into policy. The Economic Recovery Tax Act of 1981 cut marginal rates substantially, and later changes further lowered rates on capital gains and corporate income. For the Republican coalition, these moves were not merely technocratic fixes; they were a moral statement about the proper relation between the individual and the state. Over time the policy toolkit expanded beyond tax cuts to include deregulation, privatization, and a steady delegitimization of labor power. The doctrine was simple: let the incentives for capital accumulation run free and prosperity will spread.

Selling the Golden Lie: The Rhetoric and the Repetition

Any durable political story needs two things: institutional backing and narrative repetition. The trickle-down story had both. Think tanks, business associations, conservative media, and sympathetic economists amplified the message. The storyline fit everyday intuitions: people want to be the heroic entrepreneur and succeed; telling stories of the "job-creator" millionaire humanized tax cuts. The argument was packaged as both empirically sound and morally straightforward, a one-liner that crowded out more complicated, less photogenic alternatives—public investment, union power, or progressive taxation.

The narrative also exploited a psychological bias: the prospect of upward mobility. Trickle-down promised not just a better economy but a social ladder. If policy favored those who are successful today, the argument went, it would make it easier for tomorrow's innovators to climb. That promise was politically potent: many Americans hoped to be the exception—the startup founder, the high-earning professional—and so they could be made to accept policies that, in aggregate, tended to favor entrenched advantage.

Repeated often enough, simple stories calcify into conventional wisdom. Over the decades, "tax cuts for growth" became a reflexive policy prescription in many circles. It built a policy momentum that proved politically resilient—even in the face of mounting evidence that the promised benefits did not reach most people.

Reagan: The Big Experiment

Ronald Reagan was not the inventor of supply-side ideas, but his presidency was the test case. The Reagan administration's tax reforms in the early 1980s slashed top marginal rates (the top rate fell from 70% earlier in the 1970s to far lower levels during Reagan's tenure), cut capital gains rates, and pursued deregulation as a complement to tax relief. Reagan's economic program aimed to restore growth by unchaining capital. The result: a short-term recovery in GDP and a long political realignment that privileged tax-cut politics. But the tax cuts did not "pay for themselves" through massive growth; deficits rose and the distribution of income tilted upward.

What matters more than a few years of macro growth is who benefited from those years. The Reagan era marked a clear pivot: the gains of subsequent decades accrued disproportionately at the top of the income distribution. The academic picture that emerged over later decades—pieced together by studies of top incomes and wealth shares—found that the share of national income captured by the top 1 percent and top 0.1 percent rose sharply after the late 1970s and into the 1980s and 1990s. In short, the cake grew, but the slices were reallocated toward the already large slices. Scholars like

Emmanuel Saez and Gabriel Zucman have documented these shifts in painstaking historical detail.

The 1990s Interlude and the Bush Era: Consolidation of a Story

The 1990s complicated the politics. The Clinton administration raised some taxes and presided over a booming economy that produced strong revenue growth and deficits that fell—but the long-term trend of rising inequality did not reverse. Political coalitions shuffled, but the ideological frame of "growth through markets" remained dominant enough that the next substantial tax cuts—those under President George W. Bush in 2001 and 2003—were framed as pro-growth, pro-job measures. The Bush tax cuts reduced top marginal rates again, lowered taxes on dividends and capital gains, and were justified as stimulus to investment and entrepreneurship.

The empirical after-image of those decisions is instructive. The Bush tax cuts were expensive, and their benefits flowed disproportionately to high-income households. They occurred before—and in part helped create—the fiscal backdrop for the 2008 financial crisis, a crisis that reallocated wealth through bailouts and asset-price fluctuations rather than through broad-based improvements in wages or living standards. Analyses from policy groups and budget offices later documented that the tax cuts reduced the progressivity of the tax code and increased deficits—outcomes that have distributional consequences for public spending over time.

The Empirics: Profits Up, Wages Flat, Inequality Rising

The selling of trickle-down hinged on the promise that private gains at the top would translate into broad prosperity. The data tell a different story.

Start with wages and productivity. Since the 1970s, U.S. labor productivity—the output per worker—has grown substantially, but the gains in typical worker compensation have not kept pace. The divergence between productivity and median wages is one of the most robust empirical facts of recent decades: productivity rises while typical pay flattens. Economists and policy analysts have documented this "productivity-pay gap," and have pointed to policy choices—declining union density, weaker labor protections, tax and regulatory regimes favoring capital, and changes in corporate behavior—as proximate causes. The result is an economy that is more productive, with enormous aggregate output, but one where average workers have seen only modest gains in take-home pay.

At the same time corporate profits and the share of income going to capital have recovered and then surged. Firms have engaged in practices that channel earnings to shareholders and top executives—stock buybacks, dividend payouts, tax-driven profit shifting—rather than using profits to lift wages. The distributional outcome is clear: capital owners capture a growing share of national income even as typical labor compensation stagnates.

The historical arc of top income shares tells the same story. Researchers reconstructing long-run series find that the share of income accruing to the top 1 percent fell dramatically after

World War II, remained low through the 1950s and 1960s, and began rising again from the late 1970s onward. By the 1980s, 1990s, and into the 21st century, the top slices of the income pie regained—and then surpassed—the levels seen in the pre-war Gilded Age. This is not an accident of measurement; it corresponds to changes in tax policy, financialization, globalization, and political power.

These patterns are not just academic curiosities—they shape everyday life. Stagnant wages mean less ability to save and fewer resources for housing, health care, and education. Rising inequality concentrates political influence—and that concentration of influence, in turn, shapes future policy. The structural facts we observe are both cause and consequence of policy choices; they are not natural outcomes of markets alone.

Do Tax Cuts Stimulate Broad Growth? The Research Answer

One of the longest standing defenses of trickle-down is the claim that tax cuts for the wealthy stimulate investment, employment, and growth. The academic literature on this question is large and sometimes contested, but a dominant theme emerges: large tax cuts for high incomes and capital do not produce reliably outsized growth for the broader economy.

Several comprehensive reviews and empirical studies find little evidence that tax cuts targeted to the wealthy produce significant long-run increases in GDP or employment sufficient to offset their distributional costs. Analyses by mainstream institutions, including researchers at the

Brookings Institution, conclude that the evidence of major growth effects from such tax cuts is weak. Other researchers, aggregating many episodes across countries and time, find that cutting taxes on the rich tends to raise inequality but does not deliver proportional boosts in growth.

There are cases and caveats: targeted corporate-tax changes can affect investment incentives in particular sectors and regions; temporary fiscal stimulus aimed at increasing aggregate demand can boost employment in the short run. But the central claim of trickle-down—that permanent, large tax reductions for the wealthy systematically generate faster long-run growth that benefits everyone—fails to find robust empirical support. When tax cuts increase deficits, they often squeeze public investment, a channel by which long-term productivity and widely shared prosperity could have been supported.

Mechanisms: How Policy Choices Translate Into Concentration

If tax cuts for the wealthy don't reliably lift the broader economy, how do these policies function? They change incentives and redistribute economic rents through several channels:

1. Changing relative returns. Lower taxes on capital increase the after-tax return to owning financial assets, real estate, and corporate equity. That raises the value of wealth relative to wages, increasing the share of income flowing to capital owners.

2. Encouraging financial strategies that concentrate gains. Corporate governance norms shifted toward shareholder return maximization—stock buybacks, dividend payouts, and financial engineering—rather than broad investment in worker pay or productive capacity. These behaviors concentrate short-term rents in the hands of shareholders and executives.

3. Weakening public counterweights. Lower revenue from regressive tax reforms shrinks the fiscal space for public investment—schools, infrastructure, health care. At the same time deregulation or lax enforcement reduces protections for workers and consumers. The net effect is a hollowing of public goods and a reduction in bargaining power for labor, shifting more of the economy's returns toward private owners.

4. Political feedback loops. Wealth buys influence. As wealth concentrates, political power becomes skewed. Campaign contributions, lobbyists, and private networks make it easier to defend policies that benefit the already powerful. The political economy of tax policymaking itself can be reshaped by shifts in money and influence, creating a self-reinforcing cycle.

5. Globalization and tax avoidance. In an increasingly transnational economy, capital can shift across borders, and multinational firms can use tax avoidance strategies to shelter profits. Lowering domestic taxes on capital can therefore have ambiguous effects: it may reduce incentives for profit shifting, but it also leaves room for rent-seeking and jurisdiction shopping that concentrates gains among those with the means to exploit complex structures. Saez and Zucman's work on wealth accumulation and tax avoidance documents just how large this effect can be in aggregate.

These mechanisms operate together. The key point is not that tax cuts directly cause every single inequality outcome, but that these policy choices alter the incentives and balances of power in ways that favor accumulation at the top and reduce the share of growth that goes to wages and public goods.

Counterarguments and Their Limits

Proponents of trickle-down economics respond with a mix of theory and selective evidence. They point to short-term investment uplifts after certain tax reforms, to entrepreneurial dynamism, and to the idea that higher after-tax returns are necessary to fund innovation. They also argue that high taxes can discourage risk taking and reduce labor supply.

Three rejoinders are important.

First, the theoretical logic is not wrong in every case; tax policy does matter for incentives. But incentives operate inside institutions. If capital markets are deep and taxes on investment fall, some investment will occur—but the social forms of that investment matter. Investment that buys new productive capacity and employs workers is different from financial strategies that inflate asset prices or concentrate existing rents.

Second, the net macroeconomic effect of tax cuts depends on fiscal context and policy design. Many of the largest tax cuts have been paired with deficits or cuts to public investment, so even if private investment increases in some pockets, it may come at the cost of shrinking public goods that support long-run productivity. The empirical literature shows that when growth effects exist, they are often smaller than the distributional costs and uncertain politically.

Third, the political economy critique matters: the promise of a neutral, self-correcting market overlooks how tax and regulatory design can be gamed and how concentrated wealth can entrench advantage. Even if some individuals benefit from increased incentives, the broader social equilibrium—public infrastructure, democratic legitimacy, and broad-based welfare—can be damaged.

The Role of Deregulation, Unions, and Institutional Change

Tax policy is only one lever. Trickle-down as practiced was a package: tax cuts plus deregulation and a weakening of institutions that historically balanced capitalist power—especially labor unions. As unions declined, workers lost collective bargaining power that had previously transmitted productivity gains into wages. At the same time, deregulation opened new avenues for rent extraction in finance, transportation, and telecommunications, among other sectors. These combined shifts made markets friendlier to rent-seeking and less hospitable to broad-based wage growth.

Rebuilding a counterweight to concentrated power requires attention to these non-tax institutional levers as much as to tax policy: labor law, antitrust enforcement, corporate governance norms, public investment, and campaign finance rules all shape who benefits from growth. When supply-side policies were accompanied by these other changes, the combined effect was a reordering of bargaining power and a persistent widening of inequality.

Why the Golden Lie Worked Politically

If trickle-down failed as a universal growth engine, why did it survive politically? Several factors explain its durability.

First, the benefits were visible to a small but politically significant slice of the population—the rich and powerful, whose resources allowed them to reap gains and defend policies. When an idea benefits a powerful constituency, that constituency will fund think tanks, media, and lobbying to amplify it.

Second, the narrative tapped into deeply held cultural beliefs about individual responsibility and upward mobility. When an explanation for inequality frames success as pure merit and failure as personal, structural remedies appear less necessary. The trickle-down story validated both the winners and a hopeful minority who dream of being winners.

Third, the complexity of modern economies makes causal attribution difficult for the average voter. It is easier to accept a simple rule—cut taxes, grow the pie—than to navigate a complicated set of institutional reforms that require collective action, long time horizons, and politics. Simplicity is a powerful political commodity.

Finally, the design of media and political discourse tends to privilege dramatic, individualized stories of success over dry, systemic analysis. Seasonal narratives of tech founders, hedge-fund billionaires, and success stories crowd out more complicated evidence about slowly rising inequality and institutional capture. For many voters, the promise of upward mobility remains politically compelling and rhetorically potent.

Evidence Against Trickle-Down: Institutional Verdicts

Over the past two decades, a range of credible institutions and research programs have weighed in against the central claims of trickle-down. The International Monetary Fund (IMF), in detailed analytical work, has found that increases in the income share of the wealthy are associated with lower and less sustainable growth, suggesting that the benefits of concentrating income at the top do not reliably "trickle down" and may even be harmful for medium-term growth.

Similarly, comprehensive reviews of tax reform episodes find little evidence that cutting taxes on the rich produces substantial, durable boosts to growth that compensate for the distributional effects. Studies aggregated in major policy centers conclude that the growth payoff is small relative to the inequality and fiscal consequences.

These institutional findings do not settle every debate. But they are powerful: they indicate that the golden narrative—cut taxes at the top and prosperity follows—rests on selective evidence and optimistic assumptions rather than robust, generalizable empirical truth.

The Real Alternatives: Bottom-Up Growth and Shared Investment

If trickle-down is a weak or failed strategy, what works better? A growing body of evidence points toward policies that boost the incomes and bargaining power of typical workers, invest in public goods, and ensure that growth reflects broader participation. Interventions such as progressive taxation when paired with public investment in education, health, and infrastructure; policies that bolster collective bargaining and worker representation; and pro-competitive antitrust enforcement all have plausible channels to create stronger, more inclusive growth. The IMF itself has recommended policies that focus on the middle and bottom as better for durable growth.

These alternatives are not merely redistributive in the blunt sense. They are productive: better health and education produce a more capable workforce; public infrastructure reduces transaction costs and increases productivity; stronger worker voice can yield higher morale and productivity. The empirical lesson is that improving the position of the many is often better for long-run, sustainable growth than concentrating income at the top.

A Short Reckoning

Trickle-down economics was never only an economic theory; it was a political strategy and a cultural story. It promised a virtuous outcome—growth that benefits all—while supplying a convenient rationale for tax cuts and deregulation that mostly advantaged the already advantaged. The practical record is sobering: decades of policy choices that favored capital and starved public investment have coincided with rising inequality, stagnant median wages, and political dynamics that insulate power.

That is not to say that every tax cut is bad or that markets play no role in growth. The point is narrower and more urgent: policies that systematically shift resources and influence upward need to be judged by their social consequences, not only by the comfort of their rhetoric. The golden lie of trickle-down is that it offers a moral free pass for structural choices that redistribute power. In reality, redistribution is not passive. If the promise of trickle-down is to be replaced by real shared prosperity, it will require active public choices—tax policy, public investment, labor law, and institutional reforms—that are designed intentionally to broaden opportunity.

The rest of this book is about those active choices. We will unpack tools, show where they've worked and where they've failed, and try to create a pragmatic roadmap for policies that break open the piñata in ways that everyone can reach the candy. But to get there we must first stop believing a story that looks moral and feel good but does not match the outcomes. We must stop waiting for the candy to trickle. We must grab the stick.

Wealth Hoarding: How the Candy Is Stockpiled

When you picture the child at the piñata who runs forward and stuffs candy into pockets and sleeves, it looks childish — almost comical. Now imagine that child grown up, wearing a suit, operating behind layers of legal counsel, accountants, shell companies, and political influence. The behavior is the same; the scale is not. Wealth hoarding is that adult version: a set of deliberate strategies and cultural logics that remove resources from circulation, lock them into concentrated ownership, and protect them behind legal and institutional fortifications.

This chapter is a deep dive into how that hoarding happens. We'll map the toolkit used to stash candy out of sight — tax havens and shell corporations, trusts and foundations, corporate maneuvers like stock buybacks, high-end real estate and collectibles, and the legal and accounting scaffolding that makes it all appear respectable. We'll then look at why it happens: the psychology, incentives, status dynamics, and narratives (meritocracy, risk, fear) that normalize and justify hoarding. Finally, we'll trace the social and political consequences: less demand, weaker public goods, political capture, and the erosion of social trust. This is not an exercise in moralizing about individual greed. It's an explanation of how systems work — and how policy, law, and politics have made hoarding not just possible but highly profitable.

1. The Toolbox of Hoarding: Practical Mechanisms

Wealth hoarding is not one trick but many. The ultra-wealthy and their advisers use a layered, reinforcing set of tools that move money from taxable, transparent forms into opaque, privileged forms. Below are the major categories — each a familiar term, but together they form a fortress.

Offshore Accounts and Tax Havens

One of the most visible methods of hiding and sheltering wealth is offshore jurisdictions. Offshore "havens" — small states or territories with minimal disclosure requirements, low or zero corporate taxes, and secrecy laws — make it possible to park assets outside the reach of domestic tax authorities. Money can be routed through shell companies, special purpose vehicles, or trusts registered in these jurisdictions to obscure ownership and taxable events.

These practices range from the entirely illegal (outright tax evasion) to the legally dubious (aggressive tax avoidance) to technically lawful but ethically fraught arrangements enabled by gaps in international tax rules. The cumulative effect is large: estimates suggest trillions of dollars are sheltered offshore, depriving governments of revenue for public goods and social infrastructure.

Trusts, Foundations, and Family Offices

Trusts and private foundations are elegant instruments for what they are designed to do: preserve capital across generations, exert control, and provide legal protections against creditors, lawsuits, and, crucially, taxes. A properly structured trust can separate legal ownership from beneficial ownership; a foundation can maintain control over assets while extracting tax advantages.

Family offices — private firms that manage the wealth of a single family — centralize the administration of these instruments, providing sophisticated legal, tax, and investment strategies. These entities can be entirely private, immune to some public reporting requirements, and staffed by lawyers and accountants who specialize in maximizing after-tax returns and minimizing oversight.

At the same time, foundations perform real philanthropic work. The problem is the asymmetry: foundations permit families to claim public virtue while preserving private control of capital and securing tax advantages—effectively growing the treasure chest under the guise of generosity.

Corporate Tricks: Buybacks, Dividends, and Financial Engineering

Corporate behavior has changed in ways that favor concentrated ownership. One of the most notorious examples is the expansion of stock buybacks: when firms repurchase their own shares, the price of remaining shares typically rises, rewarding shareholders (and executives paid in stock). Buybacks can substitute for direct pay raises, capital investment, or research and development — and they concentrate value in the hands of owners rather than broadening it among workers.

Meanwhile, corporate finance practices — debt-financed leverage, tax-optimized profit shifting, transfer pricing — can send large flows of value toward shareholders and executives. Private equity and hedge fund structures extract fees and rents through carried interest and management fees, practices that often convert steady streams of corporate earnings into private fortunes with favorable tax treatment.

Real Estate, Art, and Alternative Assets

Real estate — particularly high-end property — functions as both a store of value and a vehicle for status and secrecy. Penthouses in global cities, luxury mansions, and even entire apartment blocks bought by investment funds can sit partly vacant while their value appreciates. Real estate offers additional advantages: legal ownership structures that can obscure beneficiaries, and the ability to borrow against property for liquidity without triggering a taxable event.

Collectibles — fine art, rare cars, wine, classic cars, jewelry — serve similar functions. Their value is often opaque, valuation subjective, and markets thin. These attributes make them attractive for both storing value and shifting wealth in ways that attract less public scrutiny.

The Tax Code and Loopholes

Arguably the most powerful tool in hoarding is the tax code itself. Tax policy shapes incentives: lower taxes on capital gains than on wages, favorable treatment of dividends, rules like "carried interest" that let investment managers pay lower rates on what are effectively compensation streams — these provisions change the relative returns on labor and capital and make accumulation easier for asset owners.

Loopholes and special provisions proliferate because they are often written by or for those with the most incentive and resources to lobby. The effect is structural: the system rewards ownership-based income over labor income, and the wealthy can reorganize their affairs to convert ordinary income into lower-taxed categories.

2. The Architecture of Secrecy: How Structures Reinforce One Another

It's tempting to treat each of the instruments mentioned above as separate tricks. In fact, they are interlocking pieces of architecture designed to maximize control and minimize exposure.

A typical path looks like this: a multinational corporation shifts reported profits to a low-tax jurisdiction using transfer pricing or royalty structures. Those profits are booked in a shell company in a tax haven. The corporate owners (or related family office) invest the proceeds in a mix of private equity, real estate, and collectibles — assets that can be housed in trusts registered in jurisdictions with strong privacy laws. Dividends and capital gains are realized under favorable tax regimes; family foundations absorb some returns in order to claim charitable status and legitimacy; family offices manage the rest, reinvesting to compound wealth.

This architecture has three crucial features:

- **Opacity:** Ownership and transactions are obscured through layers of legal entities and cross-border flows, making oversight and enforcement costly and difficult.

- **Privilege:** The legal and tax systems in some jurisdictions explicitly privilege certain forms of ownership—trusts, foundations, shell corporations—over ordinary, transparent forms of income.

- **Perpetuation:** The structure is generational. Trusts and foundations are designed to outlive any single individual, preserving control for descendants and entrapping the wealth in succession plans that avoid taxation.

These features ensure that hoarded wealth is not merely parked; it is protected and grown, often invisibly to the public that funds infrastructure, schools, and services through taxation.

3. The Incentives: Why Hoarding Is Rational (For Those Who Benefit)

It is important to step outside moral language for a moment and consider incentives. Viewed through the logic of maximizing after-tax, after-regulatory returns, hoarding is rational. The aim is simple: preserve and increase real wealth while minimizing risk and interference. Let's unpack the main incentive logics.

Security and Risk Management

Even very wealthy individuals face risks: litigation, political changes, business reversals. Structures like trusts and offshore entities are, in part, insurance. They reduce legal exposure and create buffers against policy changes or messy personal liabilities. When institutions (banks, governments) appear uncertain, the wealthy use their means to diversify and protect.

Intergenerational Transfer

Wealth is not just about consumption; it's about the power to shape future generations' opportunities. Structuring wealth to avoid transfer taxes and keep it under family control protects that influence. For parents who have benefited from their networks and advantages, the logic of "preserving the family's fortune" is compelling.

Status and Competitive Signaling

If a large part of elite life is signaling — which yacht, which art piece, which address — hoarding becomes a cultural competition. Prestige goods do social work: they mark membership in a class. Accumulating these markers signals distinction, and in social ecosystems where ties, introductions, and club memberships matter, those signals have economic value.

Incentives Created by Policy

Tax codes, corporate rules, and regulatory environments create direct incentives to reclassify income as capital, to favor corporate payouts over wages, and to seek shelter across borders. When laws are written or interpreted in ways that reward particular structures (capital gains at lower rates, carried interest treated specially), rational actors will take advantage.

The combination of personal motives (security, status, legacy) and policy-created incentives makes hoarding not merely a moral choice but an economically rational strategy for those positioned to use it.

4. The Psychology of Hoarding: Fear, Status, and the Meritocracy Myth

Beyond the cold calculus, there is a psychology that sustains hoarding. Understanding it helps explain why hoarding is not only tolerated but often celebrated in public culture.

Fear and Scarcity Mindset

Even immense wealth can coexist with a scarcity mindset — fear of loss, fear of status erosion, fear of instability. This emotional dynamic pushes accumulation beyond need. Wealth becomes a hedge not simply against economic fluctuations but against a perceived sliding scale of respect, influence, and social position.

The wealthy often fear losing their status, power, or security, even when their wealth far exceeds what they need to live comfortably."

Status, Competition, and Conspicuous Consumption

Thorstein Veblen called it "conspicuous consumption" — using visible signs of wealth to indicate social ranking. Today, that's still live. Whether through trophies (art, cars, estates) or more subtle displays (private schooling, philanthropic boards), public displays of wealth reinforce social hierarchies and justify continued accumulation. The richer you are, the more you must show it, because social position is both defended and earned through performance.

The Meritocracy Narrative as Moral Cover

If you believe your wealth is the deserved result of talent and hard work, it becomes easier to see hoarding as legitimate. The myth of meritocracy operates like moral insurance: it deflects questions about structural advantage and reframes concentration as reward rather than extraction. This narrative is powerful because it appeals to fairness and effort — values many hold dear — and it provides a moral script for keeping the candy.

Detachment and Moral Distance

Extreme wealth can create social and psychological distance from everyday realities. When wealth insulates experience — through private security, medical care, school choices, and bespoke services — empathy for public struggles erodes. Detached elites experience inequality differently, sometimes seeing redistribution proposals as theoretical threats rather than policies that could improve public life. This detachment is both cause and effect: it encourages hoarding and makes its consequences invisible.

Cognitive Dissonance and Moral Licensing

There's also a psychological trick called moral licensing: the idea that one's good deeds permit other less palatable behavior. Philanthropy can function like moral licensing. By giving a portion of wealth to charity or establishing a foundation, individuals win moral credit that can be used to justify—or distract from—continued accumulation. This dynamic doesn't negate the value of real charitable work, but it explains how philanthropy can be deployed strategically to maintain control and reputation while hoarding persists.

5. The Political Lever: How Hoarded Wealth Becomes Policy Power

Hoarded wealth doesn't stay silent. Money converted into influence reshapes policy in ways that make hoarding self-reinforcing.

Lobbying, Campaign Finance, and Revolving Doors

Wealth buys access: funding political campaigns, underwriting think tanks and media, and paying for lobbyists who write the language of law. When laws favor tax avoidance, weak antitrust enforcement, or labor-law exceptions, the wealthy have achieved policy that protects their stockpiles.

A related mechanism is the revolving door: regulators join the industries they once oversaw; executives circulate into government roles and back into corporate positions. This churn blurs boundaries, softens enforcement, and creates sympathetic interpretations of rules that favor insiders.

Idea Industrial Complex: Think Tanks and Media

Ideas matter. Wealth funds the creation of narratives: research centers, op-eds, and media operations that shape public understanding. The promotion of meritocracy, the valorization of entrepreneurship, and the persistent narrative that taxes "punish success" are all part of a communications ecosystem financed and amplified by affluent actors. These narratives help make hoarding palatable to the public and to policymakers.

Legal Capture and Regulatory Design

Laws are written with details that matter. Carried interest, step-up basis on capital gains at death, complex estate planning rules — these are technical provisions that require legal expertise to appreciate, but they profoundly affect distribution. When legal drafting is influenced by those with the most to gain, rules naturally tilt in favor of preservation of wealth. The result: a legal scaffolding that normalizes inequality and makes redistribution politically costly.

6. The Macro Consequences: What Hoarding Does to an Economy and a Polity

The tactics outlined above are not just private behaviors; they have social consequences. Hoarding reshapes economies in measurable and corrosive ways.

Reduced Aggregate Demand and Slower Inclusive Growth

Wealth hoarded at the top circulates more slowly than wages spent by households. When more income flows to the wealthy — who have high marginal propensity to save — aggregate demand can be weaker relative to potential. That dynamic depresses investment that depends on consumer spending and can reduce the incentives for firms to expand employment.

Hollowed Public Goods

When tax bases shrink because of avoidance and loopholes, public revenue available for schools, health, infrastructure, and social insurance declines. Underfunded public services create cumulative disadvantages: poorer education, worse health outcomes, weaker infrastructure, all of which reduce productivity and social mobility.

Political Inequality and Democratic Erosion

When wealth buys outsized political influence, the policymaking process skews toward narrow interests. Policy becomes less responsive to median citizens and more attuned to donors. Over time, trust in government erodes. The result is a vicious cycle: policy choices facilitate further hoarding, and hoarding deepens the political power that preserves those choices.

Social Fragmentation and Instability

Inequality breeds resentment and fragmentation. Enormous, visible differences in wealth and opportunity can produce political backlash, populist movements, and social unrest. The concentrated power of hoarded wealth makes democratic remedies harder to achieve, increasing the risk that conflict, rather than compromise, becomes the channel for change.

7. Case Studies and Illustrations (Composite and Typical Paths)

To make this concrete, imagine two composite — but representative — stories.

Family A: The Inherited Fortress

A family with intergenerational wealth centralizes assets in a family office. Trusts split legal ownership from beneficiaries; foundations are established for philanthropy and tax benefits; property is purchased via holding companies in favorable jurisdictions. The family diversifies into private equity and art, borrowing against appreciated assets for liquidity in ways that avoid sale and realization of taxable events. Political giving funds think tanks and campaigns that support tax provisions beneficial to estates. Over generations, the family retains influence and avoids substantial tax burdens while public services in their city decline.

Entrepreneur B: From Startup to Shelter

An entrepreneur grows a firm, goes public, and accumulates substantial equity. Rather than re-investing heavily domestically, the firm engages in buybacks, enriching shareholders and executives. The founder parks wealth into an offshore structure and sets up a foundation supporting causes aligned with their public image. Changes in tax law lower capital gains rates, and legal advice helps reclassify future earnings in advantageous ways. The entrepreneur benefits from public goods in education and infrastructure early on, but later uses influence to shape policy that locks in advantages.

Both paths show how hoarding is not a single act but a system of choices, incentives, legal tools, and political investments that echo across time.

8. The Moral Argument Revisited: Beyond Blame to Design

It's tempting to reduce the discussion to moral blame — the rich are greedy; the poor are victims. That's true as far as it goes. But if we want durable change, we must move from individual moralizing to institutional design. Hoarding persists because institutions permit and reward it. Change requires redesigning the incentives and closing the loopholes that make hoarding rational and politically sustainable.

Wealth hoarding is deliberate, and rightly so. Many of the mechanisms we've described are the result of policy choices, legal definitions, and political bargaining. When we treat hoarding as a system problem, we open up policy levers: tax reform, transparency rules, antitrust, campaign finance reform, public ownership, and worker empowerment. These are the sticks we will later discuss in depth; here, it is enough to note that each lever addresses a different node in the hoarding architecture.

9. Small Remedies and Their Limits

Before moving to the big solutions, a quick note on smaller reforms often proposed: closing single loopholes, imposing higher disclosure requirements, or tightening particular trust rules. These measures can produce positive effects, but they are often outmaneuvered by innovation in legal and financial markets. New instruments appear to exploit remaining seams. Without comprehensive design — international cooperation on tax, minimum global standards, and robust enforcement — piecemeal fixes risk being swallowed by adaptation.

That said, small reforms matter. Greater transparency reduces opacity, public pressure can make certain practices untenable, and narrowing egregious loopholes raises revenue and signals a change in norms. But the scale of modern hoarding suggests that systemic architecture must be addressed, not merely tinkered with.

10. Why People Tolerate Hoarding: Social Narratives and Captured Consent

Why do societies tolerate a system that visibly advantages a few ? Narratives matter. Meritocracy, market worship, and fears of "stifling" innovation produce a culture of captured consent. Philanthropy buys reputational currency and often blunts critique. Media narratives celebrate the rags-to-riches story while obscuring inherited advantage. These stories make hoarding psychologically and politically acceptable.

11. Toward Alternatives: A Preview

If the piñata is fortified by secrecy, legal structures, and political influence, then the tools to break it must attack those fortifications: transparency, tax redesign, platforming worker power, anti-monopoly enforcement, and public ownership where appropriate.

We will also need to address the psychology: changing incentives only goes so far if narratives of meritocracy and fear remain unchallenged. Mobilization requires storytelling and shared civic projects that normalize redistribution as investment rather than punishment.

12. A Short Reckoning: Facts, Power, and Possibility

Let's end this chapter with a balanced reckoning: wealth hoarding is technically sophisticated, politically entrenched, and culturally legitimated. It is also, crucially, addressable. The mechanisms are public knowledge; the policies that sustain them are the product of human choice. That means remedies are likewise feasible — but they will require political will, international cooperation, legal redesign, and cultural reorientation.

The candy inside the piñata is not finite in the sense that it cannot be shared. It is the product of collective effort: infrastructure, institutions, labor, and public order. Hoarding withdraws that product from the public sphere and concentrates access to a few. The ethics are clear: a healthy community depends on circulation — of goods, of opportunity, of power.

To stop hoarding, we must name its tools, understand the incentives behind them, and confront the narratives that justify them. This chapter aimed to do the first two. The remainder of the book will tackle the third: how to change rules, design better institutions, and build a politics capable of reclaiming the candy for the party.

Inequality by Design

The piñata isn't just hard to break because it's made of papier-mâché. It's hard because someone built a cage around it, hung it on a high hook, and threaded extra rope through the ceiling so it swings away from anyone who tries to reach it. The candy inside might be plentiful, but the architecture around the piñata — the ladder that only some can climb, the rope pulls controlled by a few, the rules about whose turn comes next — determines who actually gets to eat.

"Inequality by design" means just that: inequality is not merely an accidental outcome of markets or random luck. It is produced, reinforced, and reproduced by laws, bureaucratic rules, institutional choices, and deliberate political decisions. Lobbying writes the fine print that becomes law. Tax codes carve out privileges for some kinds of income. Zoning maps decide which neighborhoods get parks and which get highways. School funding formulas turn local property taxes into an engine for unequal schooling. Campaign finance rules let money shape elections and the rules they produce. All of these are not incidental; they are design elements that fortify the piñata.

This chapter traces how public policy and institutional design produce and polish those fortifications. We will walk through the major building blocks — lobbying and regulatory capture, tax law and loopholes, zoning and land-use policy, education funding, and campaign finance — showing how each mechanism makes the piñata harder to break and how together they form a resilient structure that preserves concentrated advantage. I want to make one thing clear up front: identifying design does not mean fatalism. Design can be changed. But to change it, you must first know how it works.

The Hand That Writes the Rules: Lobbying and Regulatory Capture

If law is the architecture of society, then lobbying is the industry of drafting blueprints. Lobbyists translate private interests into the language of policy. Sometimes that translation produces legitimate expertise — technical fixes, compliance pathways, necessary clarifications. Often, however, it produces rules that tilt outcomes in favor of those with the means to pay for drafting, persuasion, and access.

Regulatory capture — the process by which regulatory agencies come to be dominated by the industries they regulate — is a central mechanism for inequality by design. Capture can be subtle: staffing agencies with former industry executives, consulting relationships that blur the line between regulator and regulated, or simply a persistent flow of arguments and evidence that favor industry positions. When regulators treat industry preferences as defaults, rules become easier to game and harder to use for public protection.

How does capture fortify the piñata? A few patterns repeat across sectors:

- **Rulemaking that favors complexity over clarity.** Detailed, technical rules are easier for well-funded actors to exploit. Complexity creates niches for lawyers and accountants to invent avoidance strategies; it erects a cost barrier that discourages small actors from participating.

- **Enforcement weakness.** A rule that looks strong on paper but is rarely enforced functions as a paper wall. Enforcement requires resources, political will, and institutional independence. When enforcement is inconsistent, rules merely serve as window dressing.

- **Sandboxes and exceptions.** Special exemptions for "innovation" or "pilot" programs often become permanent advantages for early movers. Firms with influence lobby for carve-outs that then ossify into stable privileges.

- **Regulatory forbearance.** On issues from finance to environment, regulators sometimes step back in the face of industry claims that strict action will harm jobs or competitiveness, thereby prioritizing short-term profits over long-term public goods.

When coupled with deep pockets, access becomes influence and influence becomes durable advantage. The result is a policy environment where the favored can shape the instruments meant to discipline them.

Tax Law as Architecture: How Codes Carve Privilege

Tax law is one of the clearest examples of inequality by design because the rules directly reshape incentives and after-tax outcomes. Tax codes aren't neutral arithmetic; they embody priorities, values, and political bargains. The structure of rates, deductions, credits, and exemptions determines what kinds of income and wealth are rewarded, meaningfully shaping the distribution of resources.

Consider the following structural design choices and their effects:

Differential treatment of income

When income from capital (dividends, capital gains) is taxed at lower rates than labor income (wages, salaries), the policy privileges owners of assets over workers. This is not merely theoretical: over time, many tax systems have adopted lower rates for capital income under the argument that doing so incentivizes investment. But because asset ownership is highly concentrated, the practical effect is to channel benefits disproportionately to the wealthy.

Step-up basis and estate rules

Tax provisions that defer or erase tax liability on the transfer of assets across generations — for instance, allowing the heirs' basis to be the market value at death rather than the original purchase price — systematically reduce the tax burden on accumulated wealth. The architecture of estate and inheritance law therefore alters whether fortunes remain intact across generations or get partially redistributed.

Shelter mechanisms and carve-outs

Exemptions for certain investments, favorable treatment for carried interest, tax credits that primarily benefit owners of capital — these are design choices that create privileged tunnels through which value flows with reduced friction. Carve-outs are by nature political bargains: a sector or group asks for special treatment and, if it has sufficient influence, gets it. Over decades, many such carve-outs accumulate into a complex system that benefits the few.

Depreciation schedules and treatment of capital

Tax treatment of business investment — how quickly an asset can be depreciated, what counts as deductible, how losses are carried forward — shapes corporate behavior. If tax rules favor financial engineering over long-term productive investment, firms will increasingly allocate capital to strategies that maximize tax-efficient returns rather than productive expansion.

Enforcement and international coordination

Even well-designed tax laws can be undermined by weak enforcement, information gaps, or inconsistent international coordination. Offshore structures, transfer pricing, and profit shifting exploit differences in jurisdictional rules. When international tax architectures allow for arbitrage, national policy becomes less effective at capturing taxable income.

These design elements aren't accidental. They reflect lobbying priorities, ideological commitments, and historical bargains. They also reveal another truth: technical fixes — a rate change here, a closing of a loophole there — can help, but the underlying architecture requires careful redesign if redistribution is to be more than hairline repairs.

Zoning and Land Use: Geography as Gatekeeper

Zoning maps look like boring rectangles and lines on a municipal plan, but they are powerful instruments for shaping inequality. Land-use law decides who can build what where, which amenities a neighborhood gets, and which areas are preserved for single-family housing versus mixed-use development. The practical consequences are enormous: they influence housing supply, neighborhood density, transit patterns, and school funding, which in turn affect wealth accumulation, access to opportunity, and civic segregation.

Exclusionary zoning and the fortified piñata

One of the most consequential uses of zoning is exclusion: rules that effectively prevent the construction of multi-family housing in large swaths of cities. Single-family zoning, minimum lot sizes, and restrictions on accessory dwelling units keep housing supply artificially constrained in desirable neighborhoods. With constrained supply, property values remain high, benefiting existing homeowners (who are often wealthier) and creating barriers to entry for newcomers. Over time, property begets privilege: neighborhoods with high property values produce more tax revenue for schools, better services, and stronger political clout.

Parking minimums and sprawl

Zoning that mandates high amounts of parking, or that separates uses rigidly (industrial here, residential there), produces sprawl and dependence on cars. Sprawl increases commuting times, car ownership costs, and pollution burdens, disproportionately harming lower-income households and contributing to segregation by distance. Zoning choices determine the shape of daily life and how burdens and benefits are distributed across populations.

Historic preservation and growth control

Policies meant to preserve neighborhood character can become barriers to new housing and commercial activity. Historic districts and stringent design reviews often add time and cost to development, discouraging new entrants and preserving existing property value for incumbents. While preservation has cultural value, its interaction with scarcity can fortify privilege.

Public land decisions

Which parcels are reserved for parks, which for commercial development, which for affordable housing — these are political decisions. Public land transfers, lease terms, and development agreements can be structured to favor private developers or to produce public benefit. The design of public land policy matters because land is finite and its allocation is a crucial source of wealth.

Zoning and land use are therefore not neutral urban planning tools. They are levers that can either open access to neighborhoods and opportunity or erect durable barriers that keep the piñata hoarded by those already inside the rope line.

Education Funding: Local Property Taxes and the Reproduction of Advantage

Few public institutions shape life chances as much as schools. But the way we fund schools in many systems — often through local property taxes — embeds inequality into education. Rich neighborhoods, with high property values, generate more tax revenue for schools. Poorer neighborhoods generate less. The result is unequal inputs that feed unequal outputs: better facilities, smaller classes, and richer extracurricular opportunities in affluent districts; overcrowded classrooms and decayed infrastructure in poorer ones.

The vicious cycle of property tax funding

Because property taxes reflect local wealth, they create a feedback loop. Good schools raise property values, which generate more revenue, which further improves schools. Conversely, communities with lower property values start at a disadvantage and stay there. Interdistrict mobility, school choice policies, and private schooling often exacerbate that dynamic by enabling more privileged families to opt out of public systems.

State equalization and national variations

Some states attempt equalization — pooling resources and redistributing revenues to reduce disparities. But equalization efforts are often politically fraught and incomplete. Where equalization is weak, local funding remains a driver of inequality. Moreover, curricular differences, access to experienced teachers, and disparities in capital funding (buildings, technology) further entrench advantages.

Higher education and credentialing

Beyond K–12, the design of higher education financing — tuition structures, student loan systems, scholarship allocation — also shapes inequality. High tuition costs and the credential arms race privilege those who can pay or who have networks to access elite institutions. The accumulation of credentials then feeds into labor market segmentation and differential lifetime earnings.

Education funding mechanisms are part of the piñata's foundation. They convert geographic patterns of wealth into persistent advantages for some children and disadvantages for others. Changing those mechanics is central to any strategy that seeks to make opportunity truly wide rather than reserved.

Campaign Finance: Money in Politics as the Reinforcement Beam

If zoning maps and tax codes are the bricks of the fortified piñata, campaign finance is the crane that places them. Money in politics transfers economic clout into policy influence, making it easier for those with resources to protect rules that favor them.

Direct contributions and access

Big donors build access: they gain meetings, they secure attention from candidates, and they can influence the agenda. Even when contributions are regulated, the ability to fund advertising, run issue campaigns, or underwrite sympathetic research gives resources an asymmetrical voice.

Independent expenditures and dark money

The rise of independent expenditure vehicles and organizations that can spend large amounts without direct disclosure has created new channels for influence. "Dark money" organizations, nonprofit vehicles, and undisclosed funding sources amplify messages and support candidates or initiatives aligned with donor interests without transparent links to funders.

Bundling, PACs, and coordinated campaigns

Bundled contributions, PACs, and political action committees enable donors to aggregate and target funds efficiently. They also create organizational structures that persist beyond electoral cycles, shaping long-term policy priorities rather than episodic campaign stances.

The policy effects

The policy consequences are straightforward: candidates and officeholders respond to the voices most present in the room.

If those voices are funded by concentrated wealth, policies will, on average, be more attuned to concentrated interests. Campaign finance thus acts as a multiplier for influence: money buys visibility, visibility buys relationships, relationships shape the rules.

How the Pieces Fit Together: A Resilient System

Individually, zoning, tax law, campaign finance, and regulatory design can be critiqued and reformed. But the real power of inequality by design comes from the way pieces reinforce each other.

- **Tax advantages increase property and asset accumulation**, which in turn increases local political clout to defend favorable zoning and school funding arrangements.

- **Zoning restricts housing supply**, preserving property values and thus the tax base for schools that reproduce advantage.

- **Campaign finance translates wealth into rule-making influence**, ensuring that tax laws and zoning rules remain favorable or are adjusted to avoid redistribution.

- **Regulatory capture and weak enforcement** ensure that rules that might increase fairness are watered down or left unenforced.

Together, these mechanisms create a resilient system: change one part and the rest bends to resist the break. That explains why piecemeal reforms often fail to produce lasting redistribution. The piñata is not held together by tape in one spot; it's bound by a woven net.

Design Intentionality: Evidence That Some Choices Were Deliberate

It's important to be explicit: not every law or policy was written with the intent of producing inequality. Some were made for benign reasons, legacy constraints, or sectoral bargains. But many policies either were the result of deliberate lobbying or reflected clear tradeoffs that privileged particular groups. The difference matters politically because intentionality creates responsibility.

Consider the pattern of carve-outs: industry asks for favorable tax or regulatory treatment; it funds the research and persuasion to get it; legislatures pass the carve-out; the carve-out becomes the new normal. Over time, such bargains accrete into a system that clearly produces asymmetric benefits. That process is not accidental. It is design, even if the actors involved frame it as technical necessity.

Breaking the Design: Principles for Redesign

If inequality is by design, then the antidote is design too. Changing outcomes requires redesigning the institutional architecture in ways that reduce privilege and increase circulation. A few guiding principles can orient that work:

1. **Transparency by default.** Opacity is an ally to privilege. Transparency in ownership, campaign funding, and regulatory processes reduces the ability of the powerful to hide advantages.
2. **Neutrality and simplicity in tax design.** Complexity breeds loopholes. Simple, broad-based taxes with fewer carve-outs reduce opportunities to extract privileged treatment. Neutral tax bases are harder to gamify.
3. **Access-oriented local policy.** Zoning and land use should be evaluated not only by property value but by access to opportunity. Policies that expand housing supply near transit and jobs reduce geographic lock-in.
4. **Public financing of politics and strong disclosure.** Reducing the dependence of candidates on big donors levels the political playing field and increases accountability.
5. **Independent regulatory institutions with enforcement muscle.** Regulators need budgets, staff, and legal independence to enforce rules rather than treat them as consultation exercises.
6. **Equalizing education finance.** Funding reforms that decouple school resources from local property wealth make opportunity less contingent on address.

These are principles, not silver bullets. Implementation requires political strategy, coalition building, and careful policy design to avoid unintended consequences. But design principles give a roadmap: we can rebuild the architecture to favor shared opportunity, not concentrated hoarding.

The Political Challenge: Why Design Change Is Hard

Change is possible, but hard. Those who benefit from current designs have incentives to resist. Moreover, political fragmentation, misinformation, and cultural narratives about merit and scarcity complicate mobilization. Policymakers face tradeoffs and legitimate constraints. Voters face information gaps; many people's lives are busy and complicated; the cognitive load of deep institutional reform is high.

That doesn't make reform futile. It means strategy must be smart: combine immediate, tangible reforms that improve people's lives with longer-term institutional changes. Build coalitions that cut across demographics. Reframe redistribution as investment in public capacity rather than punishment. Use transparency to create public pressure and construct legal fences to make rollback harder.

From Fortified Piñata to Open Field

The fortified piñata is not the product of a single villain or a single law. It is the outcome of many small design choices, normed over decades, that together produce a system with built-in biases toward concentration. Naming the mechanisms — lobbying, tax codes, zoning, education finance, and campaign money — is the first step toward coherent reform.

Design matters. The structures we live inside bend incentives, shape behavior, and allocate opportunity. To rebuild toward a more equitable distribution of resources, we must become designers ourselves: changing rules, rewriting maps, rethinking financing, and creating institutions that prize circulation over hoarding.

The Illusion of Meritocracy

At parties you hear it as a compliment: "She worked so hard — she earned it." On the morning news, you hear it as explanation: "He started with nothing and became a billionaire." In boardrooms, it becomes policy intuition: "We shouldn't tax success; people earned their rewards." Meritocracy is comfortable because it promises a moral universe: rewards flow from effort and talent, so the winners deserve what they have and the losers simply need to try harder.

But comfort does not equal truth. Meritocracy, as commonly understood, is an illusion—a partial, misleading story stitched together from half-truths and omissions. It asserts a clean, individualistic line from effort to reward and neat causal closure: work hard → succeed. The reality is messier: inheritance, schooling, social networks, geographic luck, bias, and sheer contingency shape outcomes far more than the myth allows. The illusion of meritocracy does political work: it comforts winners (who gain moral license to hold onto advantage) and disempowers collective action (by making structural change seem unfair or unnecessary).

This chapter unpacks that illusion. We'll walk through how wealth and opportunity are actually distributed, how the institutions of childhood and community tilt the field, what psychological comforts the myth offers, and how the myth functions as a political technology. The purpose is not to demean striving or to deny that effort matters in particular cases. It is to show that individual stories are partial and that a society organized around the fiction of pure merit will lock in inherited advantage, attenuate solidarity, and make collective remedies harder to imagine or enact.

Meritocracy Is a Story, Not an Entity

First, language. "Meritocracy" feels like a neutral descriptor: a society where merit wins. But it is a story we tell about causality and fairness. Stories shape what we consider normal. If the dominant story is that success is deserved because of individual qualities, then policy tends to favor preserving the positions of those who have succeeded rather than correcting for structural unfairness.

Why does the story stick? It's psychologically appealing. It honors effort (a virtue most cultures prize), it offers hope to those who aspire upward, and it simplifies moral reasoning: if you succeed, you deserve your reward; if you fail, the implication is that you didn't try hard enough. For a civic culture, that is convenient. But convenience is not a good reason to let stories determine policy.

To see the limits of meritocracy, unpeel the life of a "successful" person. Peel back the familiar rags-to-riches narrative and you will often find an array of supports: a family safety net, social networks that open doors, access to credit, quality schooling, mentors, and sometimes inherited capital. Where those supports exist, they are rarely remarked upon; where they don't, the story becomes about individual deficiency.

Inheritance: The Long Shadow of Family Wealth

One of the bluntest refutations of pure meritocracy is inheritance. Money passed across generations amplifies advantage. Even when children of wealth are not personally more talented than their peers, they begin life on different ground: better nutrition, safer neighborhoods, summer enrichment, tutors, private schools, cushioned college choices, and family networks that offer internships or seed capital. Those advantages compound.

Think about the mechanisms. An inherited home in a good school district yields not just shelter but a stream of advantages: high-performing schools, local peers who are themselves advantaged, small class sizes, and alumni networks that open doors later. An inheritance can fund higher education without debt, enable risk-taking (starting a company, pursuing art), and serve as a down payment on property that will appreciate. Even modest inheritances can change trajectories dramatically.

Inheritance also shapes the psychology of risk. A family with a safety net tolerates failure; entrepreneurs with fallback capital can pivot after mistakes. Those without that safety net face a narrower set of choices—risk-averse jobs, fewer experiments, more pressure to earn immediately. The result is that inherited wealth is not only a transfer of money but an intergenerational amplifier of opportunity and security.

It's important to note that inheritance is not inherently evil. Families wanting to transfer advantage to their children is an understandable preference. The question is whether a system that allows large, untaxed or lightly taxed fortunes to flow across generations without compensating public investment is compatible with the values of a democratic society. Many modern policy debates turn on this point: how to balance family prerogatives with social fairness.

Unequal Schooling: Childhood Is the Hidden Curriculum of Inequality

Schools are the classic site where merit is supposed to be measured. But schooling systems are deeply unequal, and schooling itself is shaped by pre-school factors. Two children with similar aptitudes can walk into first grade with very different starting points. One has had three years of quality early education, regular meals, stimulating books and conversations, stable housing, and parent time to support homework. The other has had inconsistent care, food insecurity, crowded housing, and schools that lack basic supplies.

Funding systems matter. Where K–12 financing depends heavily on local property taxes, the geography of wealth translates into educational inequality. Schools in affluent neighborhoods have better facilities, more experienced teachers, smaller class sizes, and richer extracurricular options. Those advantages show up in test scores, advanced coursework access, and, importantly, in the cultural capital that helps students navigate institutions of higher education and the job market.

But inequality in schooling is not just about money. The "hidden curriculum" includes norms, expectations, teacher expectations, discipline practices, and exposure to extracurriculars that matter for college applications and resumes. Tracking systems—putting some kids on college-prep paths and others on vocational tracks—can harden early advantages into lifetime differences.

Higher education is not immune. Elite universities recruit heavily from certain high schools, favor legacy admissions, and provide access to networks that yield internships and first jobs in lucrative fields. Admissions processes that privilege standardized test scores without adjusting for background are another mechanism that makes merit a poor indicator of potential. The result: credentialing systems become gatekeepers that amplify social origin.

Networks and Social Capital: Who You Know Counts

Beyond money and school, social networks are a powerful engine of advantage. Jobs, promotions, funding, and partnerships often flow through informal networks. Who you know matters as much as what you know. This is not a conspiracy—networked hiring and referral-based opportunities are efficient—but they are unequal.

Consider internships and the "friend of a friend" referral for a coveted job. Affluent families who have friends in finance, tech, media, or law can arrange internships or introductions for their kids. Those internships lead to experience, which leads to full-time roles, which build resumes that then feed into more prestigious roles. Networks can substitute for formal credentials and accelerate career trajectories.

Social capital also includes norms and tacit knowledge: how to dress for interviews, how to negotiate salary, how to present oneself in elite spaces. These skills are often learned at home, in communities, and through mentors. They are not evenly distributed and, when combined with financial advantages, create a compounding effect.

Geography: The Luck of Where You Land

Where you are born matters. Geography shapes access to jobs, education, health care, and social mobility. Urban centers with dense industries, vibrant cultural institutions, and high-quality universities concentrate opportunities—if you live nearby, you can benefit from them. Conversely, people born in declining industrial towns or remote rural regions face fewer connections to fast-growing sectors, worse public services, and fewer social networks.

Geography interacts with policy. Investment in transit, broadband, and regional economic development can either amplify or mitigate geographic disparities. But absent intentional policies, geography often reproduces advantage: cities attract talent and capital, raising housing costs and excluding many; suburbs sort by income and reinforce school funding differences. The result is that location is a form of lottery: some are born into ecosystems that make upward mobility easier; others are not.

Bias, Discrimination, and Structural Exclusion

Any honest account of meritocracy must grapple with discrimination—based on race, gender, disability, sexuality, religion, and class. Discrimination manifests in hiring, promotion, pay, and credit markets. It also shows up early in life: disproportionate school discipline, differential expectations from teachers, health disparities, and over-policing in certain neighborhoods. These structural disadvantages are not individual defects; they are systematic patterns that accumulate over time.

Implicit bias—a cognitive tendency to favor people who resemble us—plays a role in evaluation. When recruiters, managers, or teachers unconsciously reward familiar backgrounds, they reproduce advantage. Formal discrimination—redlining in housing markets, restrictive covenants, workplace harassment, and discriminatory lending—has a historical and ongoing footprint that shapes who gets which opportunities.

The logic of meritocracy collapses when groups are systematically excluded or disadvantaged. If some people must overcome structural barriers that others do not face, merit becomes a poor measure of worth or potential. Meritocratic rhetoric then functions to obscure the role of exclusion and to attribute disparities to individual ability.

Luck and Contingency: The Unseen Forces

Beyond structural factors, luck matters. Random events—meeting a mentor, catching a crucial break, being in the right place at the right time—can change trajectories.

Serendipity is rarely part of public narratives of success, which prefer tidy causal chains. But randomness is real: a chance meeting at a conference, a fortunate assignment, or avoiding an accident can alter life paths.

The importance of contingency undermines the moral neatness of meritocracy. If luck plays a role in success, it's harder to claim that winners are purely deserving and losers purely blameworthy. A generous society recognizes contingency and builds social insurance and public investment to smooth the effects of bad luck while encouraging the productive role of risk-taking.

The Psychological Pull of the Myth: Comfort for Winners, Consolation for Losers

Why does the myth persist despite evidence to the contrary? Because it serves psychological and social functions.

For winners, meritocratic narratives provide moral justification. If wealth and status can be framed as deserved, then the anxiety of moral judgment is reduced. Success becomes a sign of virtue, not luck or social positioning. This moral cover is important—if winners feel morally licensed, they may be less inclined to support redistributive policies.

For those struggling, the myth offers a form of consolation: if you try harder, you could be the exception. This solace is productive—aspiration can motivate achievement—but it also becomes a demobilizing ideology when structural barriers block mobility. If the narrative insists that failure is personal, people are less likely to organize collectively for institutional change.

The myth also organizes social identity. People locate themselves on narratives about deservingness: "I worked for what I have" or "they simply made poor choices." These identities shape how people evaluate policy: redistributive proposals feel like an affront to fairness if fairness is defined narrowly by individual deserts.

Meritocracy as a Political Technology

The cultural functions of the meritocracy myth have political consequences. When social outcomes are framed as deserved, policy debates narrow: redistribution looks like punishment for success rather than correction for systemic distortion. The myth thereby reduces the political imagination: if everyone has an equal shot, why change the rules?

Powerful actors exploit this political architecture. They tell stories of entrepreneurship and self-made success while downplaying structural supports. They fund think tanks, media narratives, and school reforms that emphasize individual responsibility over public provision. The effect is to shift the burden of explanation from social structure to individual character.

At the same time, the myth is used to justify policies that preserve advantage: lower taxes on capital as reward for "risk," privatized education as meritocratic sorting, deregulated labor markets as incentives for work. Each policy then becomes framed as promoting merit, even when its practical effects are to consolidate advantage.

The Costs of Believing the Myth

Belief in a pure meritocracy carries costs—economic, social, and political.

Economically, it discourages public investment in shared infrastructure (schools, health care, transit) because such investments are framed as inefficient or as rewarding the undeserving. Politically, it narrows the scope for progressive reforms. Socially, it erodes solidarity; if people see inequality as deserved, they are less likely to support redistribution or to empathize with others' struggles.

Moreover, belief in meritocracy can produce perverse behaviors among winners: overconfidence, risk-seeking without accountability, and a preference for private solutions (private schools, private security) rather than public goods. That withdrawal further erodes the public realm and deepens fragmentation.

Reframing Merit: From Individual Test to Social Condition

If the meritocracy story is inadequate, what should replace it? Not nihilism or dismissal of effort, but a more honest accounting: that individual achievement is real but always embedded within social conditions. Merit should be reframed as a two-part judgment: personal effort plus fair access.

Imagine rewarding effort in a context where everyone has a reasonable baseline of education, health care, and security. That changes the meaning of merit: it is not an absolute metric detached from context, but a relative one judged within a fair field. Meritocracy then becomes a goal of equal opportunity—ensuring that personal talent has a fair chance to translate into success.

This reframing changes policy priorities. It shifts emphasis from rewarding outcomes (e.g., high incomes) to investing in inputs and leveling fields: early childhood education, equitable schools, unbiased hiring practices, paid family leave, and robust anti-discrimination enforcement. It also reframes taxation: not as punishment for success, but as collective investment in the public conditions that make success meaningful and broadly accessible.

Democratic Implications: Solidarity, Agency, and the Possibility of Change

Belief in pure merit undermines the civic glue of democracy; belief in fair opportunity reinforces it. Democracies thrive when citizens perceive a common stake and when institutions are seen as responsive to broad interests. The illusion of meritocracy undercuts both: if people believe the system is fair in principle but observe unfair outcomes, cynicism grows—"the game is rigged"—and political disengagement or populist backlash can follow. Alternatively, if citizens know the system is imperfect but also see plausible paths to improvement—investments in schools, anti-corruption measures, fair taxation—they have reason to participate constructively.

Collective action is not just about redistribution; it is about building institutions that make merit meaningful. Workers organized for better wages, parents organized for better schools, and communities organized for cleaner air are not asking to punish success; they are demanding a social baseline that converts individual initiative into broadly shared gains.

Practical Steps: Reducing the Myth's Power

If the illusion of meritocracy is politically and socially harmful, what practical steps weaken it and create a healthier, more accurate public narrative?

1. **Transparency about origins of advantage.** Public discourse should make visible the structural sources of advantage—inheritance, school funding, tax breaks. Storytelling matters: journalism, civic education, and cultural narratives that show how outcomes arise from networks and institutions can shift public understanding.
2. **Invest in common goods.** Greater public investment in early childhood, schooling, health care, and transit reduces the role of family wealth in determining outcomes. Doing so doesn't eliminate effort; it amplifies the payoff to talent regardless of birth.
3. **Leveling policies in access to capital.** Small-business lending, community banks, and equitable housing policy expand the set of people who can take

advantage of entrepreneurship and investment opportunities.

4. **Reform credentialing.** Make college admissions fairer by accounting for background; expand vocational and apprenticeship pathways that reward skill without gatekeeping by elite institutions.
5. **Anti-discrimination enforcement.** Stronger enforcement and better-designed evaluation practices (blind hiring, standardized rubrics, structured interviews) reduce the bias in hiring and promotion.
6. **Progressive taxation as public investment.** Thoughtful taxation strengthens public goods that make merit meaningful; framing tax policy as shared investment rather than punishment of winners can shift public attitudes.
7. **Political reforms to shift narratives.** Public financing of campaigns, disclosure of lobbying, and civic education can democratize policy-making and make it harder for narrow interests to capture public narratives.

Each step reduces the distance between effort and outcome that the myth pretends is already small. They do not eliminate luck or human differences in talent. But they make the link between merit and reward more just and more visible.

Humility, Ambition, and a Better Story

The illusion of meritocracy is a powerful story because it flatters and simplifies. Unmasking it requires humility and moral courage. Humility, because it asks winners to acknowledge the supports that helped them succeed; courage, because it asks society to design institutions that share opportunity rather than hoard it.

Meritocracy need not be abandoned entirely; it can be rescued from idealized dogma and turned into a more honest civic aim: to create a society in which talent and effort have a fair chance to flourish. That aim is not merely moral; it is pragmatic. Societies that invest in broad capability see stronger growth, greater social cohesion, and healthier democracies. A meaningful meritocracy is not a hall of private trophies; it is a civic architecture in which people—regardless of birth—have the tools to make the most of their talents.

So let us tell a different story: one that honors effort and recognizes fairness. A story that does not ask people to believe every success is earned or every failure self-inflicted, but that builds institutions which make merit more real. The piñata can be redistributed — not by denying individual effort, but by changing the rules so everyone gets a turn at the stick.

The Broken Stick: Why Mild Reforms Fail

Imagine a child handed a splintery twig to strike a heavily wrapped, well-hung piñata. The bark flakes off. The twig bends. A small piece of candy falls and the crowd applauds. The party carries on as before; the piñata remains mostly intact. We cheer the small victory and call it progress.

That image — the broken stick — is the central metaphor of this chapter. Over and over, societies attempt small, politically palatable reforms to redistribute power or resources, only to discover the instruments they choose are too weak, too narrow, or too compromised to change outcomes meaningfully. These reforms may be sincere, may provide minor relief, and may even be necessary first steps. But if the goal is structural change — getting more candy into more hands on a sustained basis — a broken stick is worse than useless: it creates the illusion of action while leaving fortress structures intact.

We will examine the mechanics: regulatory capture and revolving doors, legal loopholes and clever avoidance, underfunded enforcement, diluted compromises and sunset clauses, and symbolic measures designed to pacify public anger. We'll analyze how political incentives favor small gestures over systemic fixes, how elite actors adapt and co-opt reforms, and how the architecture of policy-making — complexity, jurisdictional fragmentation, and resource scarcity — creates durable resistance to deep change. Finally, we'll make the case that meaningful reform requires tools designed with enforcement, resilience, sequencing, and political strategy in mind — not just rhetorical victories.

This is not an argument against reform. It is an argument for better reform: the kind that recognizes how systems respond, anticipates counter-moves, and designs durable institutions rather than optics.

1. Why a Mild Fix Often Looks Attractive

Before cataloging the ways reforms fail, it helps to understand why mild reforms are so politically and culturally attractive in the first place.

1. **Low political cost.** Small, incremental measures are easier to pass because they threaten fewer entrenched interests. Legislators can credibly claim they have "done something" while avoiding the battles needed for larger structural changes.
2. **Narrative convenience.** Leaders crave visible wins. Passing a modest law or regulation is a newsworthy moment that shows responsiveness without compelling a deeper conversation about power or systemic change.
3. **Perceived feasibility.** Complex problems are psychologically daunting. Incremental changes feel manageable — a way to move the dial without catastrophic risk. They fit the cultural preference for gradualism.

4. **Bipartisan cover.** Mild reforms can be sold as commonsense adjustments rather than ideological gambits, making them palatable across broad coalitions, or at least easier to stitch together in divided legislatures.
5. **Institutional path dependency.** Existing bureaucracies, legal frameworks, and procedural rules are built to handle modest changes. Radical redesign threatens the comfort of officials and creates substantial administrative work — a further incentive to prefer the small fix.

These factors make the broken stick seductive: it gives politicians, bureaucrats, and sometimes citizens a quick dose of confidence without tearing down the scaffold that produces the problem.

2. Regulatory Capture and the Revolving Door: When the Guard Is a Friend

One of the most persistent reasons mild reforms fail is regulatory capture. When the same actors who are supposed to be regulated influence or staff the agencies that write and enforce the rules, regulations designed to protect the public are often transformed into instruments of the regulated.

The mechanics of capture

- **Information asymmetry.** Industry insiders often have superior technical knowledge and provide the data regulators rely upon. Over time, regulators may incorporate industry framings and priorities rather than challenging assumptions.

- **Revolving doors.** Movement of personnel between industry and government creates relationships and loyalties that affect impartial enforcement. An official who expects future employment in the private sector may hesitate to impose penalties on prospective employers.

- **Resource imbalance.** Regulated industries possess the money to hire lawyers and lobbyists who influence rule development. In contrast, public interest groups and affected communities often lack the resources to match that participation.

- **Regulatory complexity.** Complex rulebooks create niches where industry specialists thrive. Overly technical requirements can be written in ways that favor incumbents who can afford compliance systems.

Why capture breaks sticks

A regulation that looks strong on paper can be implemented with a soft hand. Penalties are lowered, compliance timelines extended, reporting thresholds set high, and enforcement budgets starved. The visible structure of law remains, but the substance is hollowed out. The public sees a regulation and assumes protection; industry experiences a manageable compliance burden and continues business as usual. The twig remains broke; the piñata intact.

3. Loopholes, Legal Arbitrage, and the Multiplication of Evasion

Any well-crafted rule invites creativity. Lawyering and financial engineering are survival skills for well-resourced actors. When government imposes a limit, actors find a way around it — and sometimes the law itself helps by being incomplete, ambiguous, or siloed across jurisdictions.

Loopholes are features, not bugs

Legislative compromises often include carve-outs that, intentionally or not, create loopholes. Complex tax systems, for example, accumulate dozens of special treatments that benefit particular industries or activities. Once one loophole is closed, legal teams hunt for another. This is not merely a cat-and-mouse game; it is an industry of tax avoidance, regulatory circumvention, and jurisdiction hopping. Every new compliance cost spawns an enterprise designed to reduce it.

Jurisdictional arbitrage

In an interconnected world, actors can shift activities across borders to exploit regulatory differences. A country-level reform may look robust domestically but leave loopholes for multinational entities to reroute profits or restructure ownership. Even within countries, fragmented responsibilities — municipal, state, federal — allow actors to find the path of least resistance.

Example dynamics

- A financial transaction tax intended to dampen speculative trading prompts the creation of new derivatives that evade the tax base.
- An anti-corruption law requiring disclosure of certain payments drives the use of intermediaries and complex ownership chains that obscure true recipients.
- A subsidy cap on one program leads firms to seek subsidized financing in adjacent programs not covered by the cap.

Loopholes are not accidental side effects; they are predictable responses when policy design does not account for incentives and adaptive behavior.

4. Underfunded Enforcement: Rules Without Teeth

Even well-designed rules fail if the institutions that enforce them lack resources. Enforcement is expensive. It requires staff, data systems, legal capacity, and political support. Politicians can pass laws with glamorous names and promise enforcement, but ongoing budgets and administrative independence are the real determinants of whether a rule matters.

Why enforcement budgets lag

- **Short-term fiscal pressures.** Funding enforcement agencies competes with visible public services (schools, roads, health). Politicians under pressure may prioritize projects with more immediate voter appeal.

- **Political signaling.** Politicians can advertise new laws without enduring the conflict of sustaining enforcement; they gain credit without paying the recurring political cost of robust application.

- **Agency capture and demoralization.** Agencies starved of resources get demoralized personnel, high turnover, and loss of institutional knowledge; they become less likely to investigate complex malfeasance.

The consequences

A regulatory framework without enforcement becomes a compliance theater. Firms and actors calculate the expected penalty relative to the benefit of noncompliance; if penalties are unlikely, lenient, or hard to collect, the incentive to comply weakens. For example, a fine that is a small fraction of ill-gotten gains is merely a cost of doing business.

5. Diluted Compromises: How Political Bargains Neutralize Reform

Politics is the art of the possible — and that art often means watered-down policy. To build a coalition broad enough to pass a law, reformers adopt concessions that preserve core privileges of influential constituencies. Those concessions can neutralize effectiveness.

The dilution path

- **Sunset clauses.** Politicians add expiration dates to placate opponents, which gives industry time to adapt and plan for the end of regulation or for later repeal.

- **Phase-ins.** Gradual implementation gives firms a transition period, but it also gives them the time to restructure, lobby for further extensions, or game compliance by shifting activities temporally.

- **Exemptions and carve-outs.** To win swing votes, legislators exempt specific firms, sectors, or activities from regulation. These carve-outs can apply to the very actors most likely to be dominant, allowing them to remain advantaged.

- **Weak metrics and reporting thresholds.** Rules are designed with reporting triggers that are above common scales of activity, or with vague metrics that are hard to audit, reducing the number of entities that actually fall under scrutiny.

The political logic

Politicians often prioritize passing a law over preserving its integrity. A headline about reform is politically valuable, and the path of least resistance is to accept compromises that secure enactment. The political calculus favors small, symbolic victories because they produce immediate political capital without courting the larger conflicts that systemic reforms require.

6. Symbolic Measures and the Pacification Effect

Symbolic measures are policies that are more about signal than substance. They are visible, easy to explain, and low-cost politically. But they can function as safety valves that release social pressure without changing structural dynamics.

Why symbolism works as pacification

- **Psychological closure.** When a leader signs a law with fanfare, the public feels heard. The symbolic act reduces outrage and can dampen mobilization.

- **Political cover.** Elected officials can point to legislative accomplishments and claim responsiveness, deflecting deeper scrutiny.

- **Strategic inertia.** Once public attention fades, policy elites and regulated actors resume business as usual. The moment of symbolic change is gone; the underlying incentives remain.

Examples of symbolic measures

- Passing a code-of-conduct without oversight mechanisms.

- Mandating voluntary corporate reporting rather than enforceable disclosure.

- Creating advisory councils filled with industry representatives instead of independent experts.

- Enacting token consumer protections with weak penalties.

Symbolic measures often feel like progress because they are visible and easy to explain. But they can be corrosive when they replace honest debates about the need for structural change.

7. The Adaptive Power of Those Who Benefit

Actors who benefit from the status quo are not passive. They deploy resources — legal teams, lobbyists, strategic philanthropy, and public-relations campaigns — to adapt to, subvert, or co-opt reforms. This adaptability is part of why small measures fail: they are precisely the kinds of changes that powerful actors can absorb while preserving rent streams.

Tactics of adaptation

- **Regulatory arbitrage.** Shifting the form of activity to avoid covered categories.

- **Litigation.** Challenging rules in court to delay implementation or create uncertainty.

- **Captive governance.** Funding standards-setting bodies or "independent" research that steers normative frameworks in favorable directions.

- **Philanthropic framing.** Using giving to shape public narratives — e.g., framing wealth as public-spirited through foundations that set agendas and fund influential institutions.

Philanthropy as co-option

Philanthropy can be genuine public service. But it can also function as a strategic buffer: donors under scrutiny may fund public goods that absorb criticism while preserving private control over wealth and governance. By funding think tanks, universities, and media, wealthy actors can help define acceptable policy circles and terms of debate. This soft power helps them steer reforms toward solutions that preserve their interests.

8. Fragmentation and Coordination Problems

Systemic problems often span multiple jurisdictions and policy domains. A reform aimed at one domain — say, corporate tax reform at the national level — may be undermined by local zoning, international tax rules, or sector-specific regulations. Fragmentation creates coordination problems that weaken systemic impact.

Examples of fragmentation

- **Multi-level governance.** National reformers face subnational resistance (states, provinces, cities) that can undercut policy by offering competing incentives or enacting contrary rules.

- **Sectoral silos.** Agencies with narrow mandates lack the authority or incentive to address cross-cutting issues, such as how financial policy intersects with housing and labor markets.

- **International mismatches.** National measures to tax mobile capital can be evaded via offshore structures in jurisdictions beyond domestic reach.

The result

Reformers must build coalitions across levels and sectors — a complex and costly political task. Without such coordination, piecemeal wins are absorbed into an adaptive system that preserves aggregate outcomes.

9. The Time-Scale Mismatch: Politics vs. Institutions

Political cycles are short; institutional change often takes long. Elected officials whose horizons are months or a few years prefer reforms with immediate political payoffs. Institutional reform — building robust enforcement, creating new legal regimes, coordinating internationally — takes years or decades. This mismatch produces a bias toward reforms that deliver fast optics and away from those that build durable capacity.

Short-termism in budget and policy

Because budgets are annual and political attention fleeting, maintenance funding for enforcement or institution-building is under pressure. A new law gets passed, but without the sustained appropriations to staff agencies, the law lives on paper. Over time, collapses occur: enforcement weakens, expertise dissipates, and reform momentum fades.

10. The Role of Public Opinion and Media Cycles

Public attention shapes what reforms are possible. Media cycles move quickly; scandals produce demands for action but attention wanes. Reformers face a strategic choice: propose ambitious, technical changes that require sustained debate, or propose simple, visible measures that can be passed quickly. The latter often wins. Moreover, opposition actors exploit media fragmentation to magnify uncertainty and delay reforms via litigation and PR campaigns.

Attention scarcity

Deep institutional change requires sustained public pressure. When attention is scarce, symbolic measures that can be passed quickly are appealing. But as we've argued, symbolic gestures without enforcement often pacify the public rather than redress the underlying malfunction.

11. Why Some Reforms Succeed: Lessons from Durable Change

Not every reform fails. Understanding successful cases helps illuminate what broken-stick reform lacks.

Ingredients of durable reform

1. **Clear, enforceable rules.** Laws with precise requirements, strong penalties, and clear standards reduce ambiguity and close loopholes.

2. **Adequate resourcing.** Agencies charged with enforcement must have budgets, staff, and technical capacity.
3. **Political coalitions.** Durable reform often emerges from broad coalitions — labor, business segments that benefit from fair competition, civic organizations, and political actors — that can withstand targeted pushback.
4. **Phased design with transition safeguards.** Sequencing matters: reforms that provide clear timelines, but also close evasion pathways contemporaneously, reduce adaptation windows.
5. **International cooperation when necessary.** For cross-border problems, coordinated agreements (tax treaties, information sharing) limit arbitrage.
6. **Independent oversight and judicial backing.** Independent audit and judicial mechanisms deter capture and ensure legal durability.

Case patterns

Where these elements align, reforms have a better chance. For example, progressive land-use reform that couples local regulatory changes with funding for affordable housing, clear enforcement, and political buy-in from local stakeholders can produce durable change. Similarly, tax reforms that pair rate changes with enforcement investments and international information exchange can close avenues for profit shifting.

Durable change is complex and often requires compromise — but crucially those compromises are not the kind that render rules hollow. Instead, they design around adaptation.

12. Designing Stronger Sticks: Principles for Resilient Reform

If broken sticks prevail when design ignores system dynamics, what principles produce stronger tools?

1. **Anticipate adaptation.** Policy design must model likely evasion responses and build countermeasures. That means simplicity where possible and closing alternative escape routes where necessary.
2. **Invest in enforcement.** Laws should be accompanied by realistic budgets and independent enforcement mechanisms whose funding is insulated from short-term politics.
3. **Limit capture vectors.** Create cooling-off periods for industry-to-regulator moves, transparency requirements for lobbying, and participatory rulemaking that balances expertise with public-interest voices.
4. **Use carrots and sticks.** Combine penalties with incentives for compliance to lower resistance while maintaining consequences for evasion.
5. **Coordinate across jurisdictions.** Build coalitions across local, national, and international levels to prevent jurisdictional arbitrage.
6. **Embed evaluation and iteration.** Treat reforms as experiments with mandates for evaluation,

adjustment, and tightening over time rather than one-off acts.

7. **Make transparency the default.** Reduce opacity in ownership, political spending, tax rulings, and regulation-writing to raise the reputational and legal costs of evasion.
8. **Build public coalitions.** Strengthen civic capacity for oversight — watchdogs, investigative journalism, and community organizations that can sustain pressure.
9. **Sequence strategically.** Implement reforms in an order that prevents easy circumvention: e.g., close tax loopholes while reforming rates, or upgrade enforcement while phasing in new reporting rules.
10. **Guard against sunset traps.** Resist time-limited measures that give actors time to reorganize; if sunsets are used, pair them with review mechanisms and enforcement ready at the moment of greater stringency.

These are not purely technocratic prescriptions; they are design principles that recognize politics, incentives, and human adaptation.

13. Political Strategy: How to Win Durable Reform

Technical design must be married to political strategy. Winning durable reform requires narrative framing, coalition building, and tactical sequencing. A few strategic considerations:

- **Frame reforms as investments, not punishment.** Emphasize public returns — better schools, safer neighborhoods, more stable markets — rather than moralizing winners.

- **Identify and court allies inside the private sector.** Some businesses benefit from level playing fields and can be allies against rent-seeking incumbents.

- **Use transparency to mobilize public sentiment.** Make the mechanics of evasion visible: case studies and stories humanize abstract problems and sustain pressure.

- **Create durable institutional anchors.** Enact constitutional or statutory protections for enforcement funding and independence where possible.

- **Pair popular short-term wins with long-term structural change.** For example, combine wage hikes or benefits that immediately help workers with longer-term tax and antitrust reforms.

Politics is messy. But durable reformists succeed by planning both the legal architecture and the social and political coalitions that will defend it.

14. A Short Reckoning: When Small Wins Matter — and When They Don't

We must be careful not to throw the baby out with the bathwater. Small reforms matter — they can relieve suffering, shift norms, and build capacity. For example, a modest increase in minimum standards for workplace safety can save lives. A transparency requirement that discloses political donors can reveal patterns that catalyze larger reform. Small wins can be stepping stones.

The danger is in mistaking these steps for completion. Celebrating a symbolic victory as if it solved the underlying problem is the broken-stick trap. The political class can use minor changes to absorb energy and prevent deeper structural reform. Effective reformers treat modest wins as parts of a larger strategy — leverage points rather than endpoints.

15. Toward Sticks That Last

The world of policy is contested and adaptive. Actors respond; systems realign. If reformers fail to design with that reality in mind, their measures become theater. The broken stick is not merely a failure of will; it is a failure of design: to anticipate adaptation, to invest in enforcement, to coordinate jurisdictions, and to build political defenses.

To break a fortified piñata you need more than force: you need the right tool, used by organized hands, planned with an eye to the structure that holds the candy. That is the lesson here. Mild reforms are sometimes necessary and sometimes useful — but if they are the only effort, they become a pacifying ritual. The candy remains inside.

The rest of this book turns toward better tools and strategies: sticks crafted for resilience, governance reforms that reduce capture, tax and regulatory redesign that anticipates avoidance, and political strategies that build defending coalitions. The goal is not merely to swing harder, but to change the game — to redesign the architecture so the piñata cannot be fortified again.

What Is Piñata Economics? — A New Framework

When people ask, "So what is Piñata Economics, exactly?" they usually mean two things at once: (1) what is the idea at the conceptual level, and (2) what does that idea imply in practice? This chapter answers both. It puts a stake in the ground: Piñata Economics is a practical, normative, policy-oriented framework that treats persistent inequality as the predictable result of intentional design choices and therefore as a problem that can — and must — be addressed directly. It is a manifesto and a map: a set of principles for justice, an ethical orientation toward corrective public action, and a tactical program for how to reorganize institutions so the benefits of modern economies flow more broadly.

We will define the framework formally, articulate its core principles, explain its ethical foundations (it is corrective, not punitive), delineate the scope of the changes it calls for, and show how the framework translates into measurable goals and concrete policy directions. This chapter is the spine of the book: other chapters are the tools, the case studies, and the tactical playbooks; here we set the values and the logic that justify using those tools.

1. A one-sentence definition

Piñata Economics: a political-economic framework that diagnoses contemporary inequality as the product of deliberate institutional design and adaptive rent-seeking, and prescribes an active, enforceable program of redistribution and institutional redesign — using targeted public investment, democratic governance, progressive taxation, labor empowerment, competition policy, and transparency — to restore broadly shared prosperity, democratic legitimacy, and durable opportunity.

Each clause in that sentence matters. "Diagnoses" — because we begin with an explanation of cause, not only symptoms. "Deliberate institutional design" — because rules, not chance, structure outcomes. "Active, enforceable program" — because redistribution cannot be a passive byproduct of growth; it must be intentional. The instruments named at the end are the practical levers; we will return to them throughout the book. But first the principles.

2. Core principles of Piñata Economics

The framework rests on four interlocking principles. Think of them as axioms — assumptions that guide diagnosis and policy selection. They are not dogma; they are normative starting points that explain why some policies are favored over others.

Principle 1 — Redistribution as justice and public infrastructure

Redistribution is not a grudging charity nor a temporary fix: it is the ongoing work of building and maintaining public infrastructure — both material (schools, health systems, transit) and institutional (tax administration, competition policy, legal protections) — that enables equal dignity and opportunity. Justice here is structural, not merely retributive.

Implication: Policies should prioritize public goods and durable investments that expand capabilities across the population and that generate returns in health, education, and productivity.

Principle 2 — Direct action, not trickle-down

Redistribution must be deliberate. The belief that wealth will "trickle down" is empirically weak and politically convenient for concentrated interests. Piñata Economics insists on active instruments: progressive taxation, public investment, collective bargaining, enforceable regulation — the "sticks" and "pulleys" that move resources purposefully.

Implication: Policy design privileges instruments whose causal chain to redistribution is clear and enforceable; it distrusts vague, indirect mechanisms that rely on passive flows.

Principle 3 — Systemic solutions for systemic problems

Inequality is systemic and emergent from many interacting parts: tax codes, land-use rules, campaign finance, firm structure, platform design, international tax regimes. Treating it with isolated or symbolic fixes is inadequate. The framework calls for coordinated, cross-domain reforms that address structural emissions of inequality.

Implication: Sequencing and integration matter. Tax changes must be paired with enforcement; labor reforms must be paired with competition checks; anti-corruption rules must be paired with transparency and civic empowerment.

Principle 4 — Empower the many, not the few

Redistribution should increase the agency of broad publics — through participatory governance, worker voice, community ownership, and democratic oversight. The goal is not merely to move money around but to widen who gets to shape economic rules.

Implication: Institutional designs that strengthen civic participation (participatory budgeting, worker co-determination, public procurement with community oversight) are prioritized alongside fiscal measures.

These principles orient everything that follows. They are intentionally procedural and institutional — because Piñata Economics is about how rules are made, enforced, and defended, not merely about redistributive totals.

3. The ethical stance: corrective, not punitive

One of the first objections to any frank talk about redistribution is moral: "Are you saying we should punish success?" Piñata Economics answers emphatically: no. The ethical stance is corrective, not punitive.

Corrective justice vs. punishment

Corrective justice asks: what set of rules will restore fair conditions and ensure opportunity? Punishment asks: who must be punished for what they have done? The difference is crucial. When an individual accumulates wealth under rules that were designed or tolerated to amplify rent extraction, the ethical response is to change the rules, not merely punish individuals for taking advantage of those rules. A corrective posture focuses on system design: closing loopholes, restructuring incentives, and building institutions that make accumulation compatible with broad-based prosperity.

Reciprocity and valuation

Piñata Economics appeals to reciprocity. Those who benefit most from public goods and rule-making — stable courts, educated workforces, infrastructure, a predictable currency — have a stronger claim to contribute proportionally to maintaining and improving those goods. This is not envy; it is a civic bargain: we pool resources to create public capacity that benefits private initiative.

Dignity and fairness

Redistribution must preserve dignity. That means programs are designed so people receive support without stigma: universal or near-universal designs where feasible, respectful delivery, and clear opportunities for participation and voice.

Pragmatic humility

The framework rejects moralizing purity tests. It acknowledges entrepreneurs who create value and rewards productive risk-taking. But it insists those rewards not become instruments for unaccountable power that hollow democratic institutions. The question is not whether some should be wealthy; it is whether wealth should be insulated from democratic obligation.

4. The scope of desired change: what we aim to transform

Piñata Economics has both local and global ambitions. It is intentionally ambitious because the fortifications it diagnoses are not small. The scope includes institutional redesign across domestic policy domains and international coordination. Here is a menu of the major domains the framework intends to transform.

Domestic institutional realms

- **Taxation and fiscal policy.** Progressive income taxation, wealth measures, closing carve-outs, strengthened tax administration.

- **Labor and workplace governance.** Stronger rights to organize, sectoral bargaining, portable benefits, limits on misclassification, worker representation.

- **Competition and corporate governance.** Antitrust enforcement updated for platforms, restrictions on self-dealing, corporate fiduciary reorientation toward long-term value and stakeholder interests.

- **Public goods and services.** Universal or near-universal healthcare, early childhood education, affordable housing, public transit.

- **Land use and housing policy.** Zoning reform, community land trusts, inclusionary affordable housing, and municipal leverage over public land.

- **Campaign finance and public accountability.** Small-donor amplification, disclosure, limits on dark money, transparency in lobbying and regulation writing.

- **Regulatory design and enforcement.** Built-in anti-capture mechanisms, independent funding for enforcement agencies, participatory rulemaking.

International arenas

- **Tax cooperation and transparency.** Beneficial ownership registries, automatic exchange of financial information, a credible global minimum tax.

- **Debt architecture.** A faster, more equitable debt workout mechanism; less loan-based aid for climate adaptation.

- **Trade and intellectual property.** Rules that allow policy space for development and public-interest exceptions for critical technologies.

- **Climate justice and transfers.** Grant-based financing for loss and damage, scaled public finance for adaptation.

Each domain requires policy detail and political strategy, but the principle is straightforward: change the rules where the fortifications are heaviest.

5. Building blocks of the framework: instruments and constraints

Piñata Economics is not a wish list. It is a design language that chooses instruments for their ability to produce enforceable, systemic change. Below are the building blocks — the operational levers — and the constraints that must guide their use.

Building block 1: Progressive fiscal instruments

These include graduated income tax rates, capital-income parity, closing of carry and basis loopholes, and wealth levies aimed at the extreme top. Design choices here emphasize enforceability: broad bases, fewer special exemptions, data-driven audits, and international cooperation to reduce arbitrage.

Constraint: Without enforcement capacity and international coordination, headline rates produce little revenue. Thus fiscal design pairs with administrative investment.

Building block 2: Collective labor power

Organizing laws, sectoral bargaining, and worker ownership structures reshape income distribution from the workplace outward.

Constraint: Labor reforms must account for modern work patterns (gig, platform, subcontracting) and include portable benefits and adaptable bargaining models.

Building block 3: Competition and corporate accountability

Use merger review, break-ups where necessary, limits on vertical integration, campaign-finance restrictions, and requirements for corporate transparency and stakeholder governance.

Constraint: Interventions must be evidence-based to preserve legitimate scale economies; courts matter, so legal durability and public narrative are essential.

Building block 4: Public ownership, co-ops, and procurement

Municipal ownership of critical services, support for co-ops, and procurement policies that prioritize equitable practices redistribute value through market demand.

Constraint: Public enterprises must be governed transparently to avoid politicization and inefficiency.

Building block 5: Transparency and legal enforcement

Beneficial ownership registries, reporting, whistleblower protections, and well-funded enforcement agencies convert laws into reality.

Constraint: Privacy rights and administrative burdens must be managed; international data-sharing needs safeguards.

Building block 6: Cultural and narrative work

Framing, storytelling, education, and media strategies build the consent necessary for durable change.

Constraint: Narrative work must be honest about trade-offs and grounded in local realities.

These blocks are the practical toolkit. The framework insists on bundling them in ways that anticipate evasion, capture, and political backlash.

6. Measurement and accountability: defining success

Piñata Economics foregrounds metrics. If a framework is to be operational, it must be measurable. That is not technocratic fetishism; it is democratic accountability. Below are the primary indicators the framework uses to assess progress.

Distributional indicators

- **Pre- and post-tax income shares** for top 10%, top 1%, and top 0.1%.
- **Wealth concentration** metrics: share of national net wealth held by percentiles, wealth Gini.
- **Median and bottom-decile incomes** relative to productivity.

Opportunity indicators

- **Intergenerational mobility** metrics (earnings mobility, educational attainment by parental income).

- **Access measures**: childcare slots per 1,000 children, primary-care visits per capita, availability of affordable housing units.

- **Labor-market measures**: union coverage, bargaining coverage, share of jobs with stable hours and benefits.

Institutional integrity indicators

- **Tax gap estimates** (uncollected owed taxes).

- **Enforcement capacity** (auditors per taxpayer, inspections per regulated firm).

- **Transparency indices**: beneficial ownership coverage, lobbying disclosure completeness.

Political and democratic indicators

- **Political equality measures**: campaign-finance concentration, small-donor share, access indices.

- **Civic trust and participation**: turnout, civic association membership, public perception surveys.

Progress is measured with these indicators; the framework insists on public dashboards and iterative adjustments. If reforms do not change these metrics after reasonable lag times, they are redesigned.

7. Implementation logic: sequencing and bundling

Piñata Economics is pragmatic about politics. It requires sequencing reforms so that gains are both credible and defensible. Three basic rules guide sequencing:

1. **Enforcement-first principle.** Fix transparency and enforcement weaknesses before large tax-rate increases to reduce avoidance possibilities. A credible tax is a tax that can be collected.
2. **Visible wins early.** Deliver immediate, tangible benefits (childcare slots, wage hikes in municipalities, small-business supports) to build public support for deeper reforms.
3. **Bundle complementary reforms.** Pair labor strengthening with competition checks; pair procurement reforms with support for co-ops; pair tax changes with clear spending plans on popular services.

A common sequencing template:

- Phase A (0–12 months): transparency orders, enforcement budgets, municipal pilots (minimum wage, procurement), narrative campaign launch.

- Phase B (12–36 months): base-broadening tax changes, expansion of public services funded by early revenue, legal protections for workers, targeted competition actions.

- Phase C (36–72 months): national-level progressive tax changes and minimum wealth measures paired with international coordination, institutional embedding (constitutional/ statutory locks, independent agencies).

This sequencing anticipates countermeasures and makes it harder for opponents to neuter reforms.

8. Political strategy: building coalitions and narratives

A framework must be politically durable. Piñata Economics devotes equal attention to politics and policy. Key strategic elements:

Coalition architecture

- **Broad-based coalitions**: workers, small-business owners harmed by monopoly, parents, retirees, municipal leaders, and civic groups.

- **Cross-class appeals**: emphasize shared benefits (better transit, lower drug prices, safer communities) rather than zero-sum language.

- **Institutional champions**: mayors, local school boards, union leaders, and public-health officials who can deliver evidence of impact.

Narrative playbook

- **Values-first framing**: security, dignity, fairness.
- **Concrete storytelling**: families who gain childcare seats, workers whose wages rose, neighborhoods where housing is affordable.
- **Pre-bunking and rapid rebuttal**: anticipate opponents' scare stories and equip spokespeople with data and stories.

Defensive posture

- **Legal defense funds, research teams, and media rapid-response**: pre-empt SLAPPs, PR blitzes, and litigation strategies.
- **Institutional shields**: secure funding for enforcement agencies, anti-capture rules, and participatory oversight mechanisms.

Politics in this framework is strategic and long-term; it regards policy change as cumulative and iterative.

9. Objections, trade-offs, and the framework's responses

A robust manifesto addresses likely objections. Here are common criticisms and our answers.

Objection 1 — "Redistribution kills growth."

Response: Evidence shows that public investment in human capital, health, and infrastructure enhances productivity. Redistribution that funds public goods is a growth-enhancing investment, not a pure drag. The framework targets wasteful rents and uses revenue for productive spending.

Objection 2 — "You'll send capital fleeing."

Response: Capital flight is real but manageable. Transparency, withholding mechanisms, international cooperation, and sequencing (enforce first, then raise rates) reduce the flight risk. Moreover, many investments are location-specific and depend on functioning domestic markets; stable, predictable taxation can be more attractive than ad-hoc low-tax sheltering.

Objection 3 — "People will game the system."

Response: Expect adaptation. That is why the framework pairs rules with enforcement, transparency, and multi-jurisdictional coordination. Game-resistant design uses simplicity, broad bases, and anticipatory lawmaking.

Objection 4 — "This is ideological."

Response: Piñata Economics is explicit about values, but its policy choices are pragmatic and evidence-driven. It insists on measurables and iterative correction — not theology. Programs that fail metrics are revised.

10. Institutional safeguards: making gains stick

No manifesto is complete without proposals for lock-in. Piñata Economics recommends several institutional safeguards:

- **Protected enforcement funding:** multi-year appropriations for tax agencies, competition authorities, and labor-inspection bodies.

- **Transparency law permanence:** legal entrenchment of beneficial ownership and campaign-finance disclosure so they are harder to repeal.

- **Participatory governance:** statutory rights for public input (citizens' assemblies, participatory budgeting) that create civic ownership of programs.

- **Anti-capture mechanisms:** cooling-off periods for regulators, full disclosure of lobbying, and public audit mandates.

- **Sunset-review discipline:** when time-limited policies are used, include automatic evaluation, public reporting, and criteria for renewal that make rollbacks politically costly if benefits are evident.

These safeguards are part of the framework's institutional design logic: build durable capability to keep the piñata from being re-fortified.

11. The moral imagination: why this matters beyond numbers

Piñata Economics is unapologetically political because redistribution is a political act. But it is also moral. A society that tolerates vast, durable inequality while underinvesting in common capacity is not only inefficient — it is less humane. Restoring a balance between private reward and public obligation nurtures social solidarity, improves collective resilience to shocks (economic, epidemiological, climate), and broadens the canvas of human flourishing.

The manifesto claims that how we design institutions reveals what we value. If we choose simplicity and enforcement over secrecy and loopholes; if we prefer worker voice to unilateral managerial power; if we treat care and education as shared commitments rather than market commodities — then we will get a different kind of economy. This is not utopia. It is a design choice anchored in day-to-day practice.

12. Closing the manifesto: a short program of action

Piñata Economics asks for three kinds of work from anyone who agrees with its core proposition: think, build, and defend.

- **Think:** adopt systems thinking. When assessing policy, ask how it affects distribution, enforcement, and institutions across time and space. Demand metrics and transparent evaluation.

- **Build:** prioritize the enforcement first, demonstrate quick wins, and build participatory institutions that give people voice and ownership. Use the sticks — progressive taxes, labor empowerment, antitrust, procurement, public investment — in bundles rather than as solos.

- **Defend:** anticipate counterattacks. Fund legal defenses, cultivate media capacity, and design laws with anti-capture features.

Finally, the core moral claim: people deserve a fair shot at agency and prosperity; institutions can be designed to deliver that. Piñata Economics is at once a diagnosis and a roadmap: it tells you what is wrong, why it is wrong, and — crucially — how to change it. The rest of this book supplies the tools, case studies, and political templates; this chapter gives the reason and the standards by which to judge them.

Take this framework as a working hypothesis, not a catechism. Use it to test policies, to design institutions, and to judge whether a reform truly widens access and agency. If it does, it belongs in the Piñata Economics toolkit. If not, revise.

Breaking the Piñata: Historical Wins

"We didn't get our rights by asking." That blunt sentence captures much of the history this chapter surveys. Redistribution — meaningful redistribution that changes who has power and who benefits — rarely arrives gently. It arrives through conflict, convulsion, compromise, and creativity. This chapter is a tour of precedent: moments when concentrated wealth and entrenched advantage were pushed back, and public goods and broader access gained ground. We look at labor victories (the eight-hour day, the rise of industrial unions like the UAW), New Deal and postwar programs, the high-tax, high-public-investment decades, Nordic social democracy, land reforms, and episodes of reparative justice and revolution. For each case we ask: what worked, why did it work, what went wrong, and what lessons should reformers carry forward?

This is not a nostalgic laundry list. It's a pragmatic excavation of tactics, political conditions, institutional design, and limits. These episodes show that piñatas can be pried open; they also warn about fragile gains, backlash, and the importance of enforcement and institution-building. Read this chapter as a historian and a mechanic: note the tools, their uses, and the maintenance they require.

1. The Labor Movement: Eight Hours, the UAW, and the Power of Collective Bargaining

If redistribution is a machine, unions are one of its primary wrenches. Labor organizing is how workers convert dispersed vulnerability into concentrated bargaining power.

The eight-hour movement: a century of struggle

The demand for an eight-hour day predates the 20th century but was a cornerstone of labor politics from the late 1800s through the early 1900s. In many countries, the drive for an eight-hour day fused with broader demands for worker dignity and political recognition. The fight took many shapes — strikes, political lobbying, and sometimes violent repression (Haymarket in Chicago in 1886 is a well-known flashpoint).

Why did the eight-hour day matter? It reallocated time — the most basic human resource — from the employer's control into the worker's life: rest, family, civic participation, and education. With standardized hours came predictability and, crucially, a platform from which to bargain for wages, safety, and benefits.

Key lesson: **institutionalizing norms matters.** The eight-hour day became durable when codified into law or collective agreements. Rituals like Labor Day and an organized union presence in workplaces made the right visible and enforceable.

The United Auto Workers: mass organization and industrial leverage

The UAW's rise in the 1930s is a textbook case of how concentrated, coordinated action across a dominant industry can redistribute power. The sit-down strikes in Flint, Michigan (1936–37) are emblematic: workers halted production in plants by occupying them. These strikes made leverage immediate — if the factory stopped, the employer lost the revenue and the national supply chain stalled.

The UAW's success came from multiple factors:

- **Strategic concentration.** Automobile manufacturing was centralized in a few massive plants. Workers' withholding of labor had outsized economic impact.

- **Political opening.** The New Deal era, including legal protections for collective bargaining (the National Labor Relations Act of 1935), created legal cover and political openings for unionization.

- **Tactical innovation.** Sit-down strikes and community support networks (food, housing) sustained long actions.

- **Institutional embedding.** Once recognized, the UAW negotiated contracts that redistributed earnings (wages, pensions, benefits) and set industry standards that ripple through related sectors.

Lesson: **scale and leverage matter.** Organizing a critical node in the economy — whether a port, a factory, or a logistics hub — can yield outsized gains. The UAW also shows the importance of legal protections and political coalitions.

The limits and the rollback

Union density peaked mid-century in many countries and then fell in the decades that followed. A combination of globalization, deindustrialization, employer anti-union strategies, and legal constraints eroded bargaining power. The lesson for contemporary organizers is not to romanticize the past but to translate the core principle — concentrated bargaining in strategic sectors — into new contexts (care, logistics, platform work).

2. The New Deal and the Rise of Social Insurance

The Great Depression produced policy change on a scale rarely seen: public works, social insurance, labor rights, and financial regulation. The New Deal (Franklin D. Roosevelt's program of the 1930s in the United States) is often presented as an archetype of how crisis opens policy space.

What the New Deal did

Key elements included:

- **Public employment programs** (Civilian Conservation Corps, Works Progress Administration) that created jobs and built infrastructure.
- **Banking and financial regulation** (Glass-Steagall, Federal Deposit Insurance) to stabilize the system and protect ordinary savers.

- **Social insurance** (Social Security Act of 1935), which introduced pensions and unemployment insurance as collective, contributory programs.

- **Labor law** (Wagner Act) that guaranteed collective bargaining rights and created an institutional framework for unionization.

Why did redistribution follow? The Depression's scale made mass suffering visible and politically salient. A broad coalition — labor, progressive intellectuals, municipal officials, and parts of business that benefited from stability — supported systemic interventions.

Lesson: **crises create windows.** The political feasibility of interventions often depends on perceived emergency and a sense that failure to act risks systemic collapse.

The New Deal's institutional durability and limits

Many New Deal programs endured and shaped the postwar settlement. But the New Deal was also constrained: it codified some racial exclusions (e.g., agricultural and domestic workers were largely left out of Social Security initially), and the politics of race and region limited redistributive ambition in certain areas.

Lesson: **design matters for inclusion.** Programs enacted in crisis can institutionalize exclusions if not carefully crafted; attention to reach and equity must be explicit.

3. Postwar Progressivity: High Tax Rates and Public Investment

The decades after World War II provide a striking example of redistribution on a national scale. In many advanced economies, top marginal tax rates were very high, coupled with robust public investment in education, housing, healthcare, and infrastructure. The result was high growth with broadly shared gains — what some call the "Golden Age" of capitalism.

Tax progressivity and the social compact

In the United States, top marginal tax rates were above 90% for decades after the war (nominally — with numerous deductions affecting the effective rate but the headline mattered politically). Similar patterns held in Canada, much of Western Europe, and elsewhere, combined with strong unionization in many sectors.

What drove this? Wartime fiscal practices, political consensus about reconstruction, and powerful parties and governments committed to social investment. The Marshall Plan, public housing, the GI Bill (which expanded access to education and homeownership for returning veterans), and active industrial policy in some countries contributed.

Lesson: **political coalitions with a clear narrative about shared sacrifice and investment can sustain progressive fiscal systems.** Another ingredient was lower capital mobility (capital controls), which gave governments room to tax and invest without immediate capital flight.

Growth and redistribution together

The postwar system counters two common myths: that redistribution necessarily kills growth, and that high taxes always repel investment. When public investment built human capital and infrastructure, productivity rose. Universal schooling, broad health coverage, and stable industrial relations supported mass consumption and innovation.

Caution: the compact depended on particular historical conditions — limited financial globalization, wartime state capacity, and relatively strong labor parties. As globalization intensified, policy space narrowed.

4. Nordic Models: Social Democracy, Equality, and Economic Dynamism

The countries of northern Europe — Sweden, Norway, Denmark, Finland — are often offered as models of redistribution that work. High taxes, strong social insurance, active labor market policies, and a dense public sector combine with dynamic private markets to produce high levels of social equality and strong indicators of well-being.

The institutional anatomy of the Nordics

Key features:

- **Universal social insurance.** Childcare, healthcare, parental leave, pensions — broadly universal and generous.

- **Active labor market policy.** Strong retraining, public employment services, and programs that smooth transitions.

- **High union coverage combined with flexible labor markets.** The "flexicurity" model (often associated with Denmark) mixes generous benefits with flexible hiring and firing, underpinned by strong retraining systems.

- **Broad public investment and progressive taxation.** Financing is via high, progressive taxes combined with efficient administration.

Why did this work? Political coalitions formed after World War II that trusted public institutions, had effective social dialogue among unions, employers, and the state, and invested in public goods that enhanced productivity. Small population size and homogenous institutions sometimes get cited as facilitating consensus, but that's an incomplete story: the Nordic model also required contested politics and continual bargaining.

Lesson: **redistribution that invests in capability and pairs social protection with labor market dynamism can sustain competitiveness.** The institutional detail — active retraining, strong public services, and shared governance — matters as much as headline tax rates.

Caveats and adaptations

Nordic systems are under pressure from demographic change, migration, and global competition. The lesson is not "copy Stockholm wholesale" but to adapt the principles — universal access, social investment, labor voice, and institutional trust — to local conditions, politics, and administrative capacity.

5. Land Reform: Redistributing the Ground Beneath Our Feet

Land reform is a blunt but historically transformative redistribution tool. By breaking feudal or oligarchic land ownership, countries have restructured rural power and shifted the distribution of wealth.

Japan and South Korea: postwar land reform success

After WWII, both Japan and South Korea implemented land reforms with significant redistributional effects. Japan's occupation authorities and domestic reformers used purchase and sale schemes and legal changes to transfer land to tenant farmers. South Korea followed with extensive reform in the late 1940s and 1950s.

Why effective? Land reforms created a broad base of smallholders with vested interests in stability and consumption — a foundation for mass markets, rural development, and social stability. Importantly, reforms were sometimes paired with credit access, extension services, and supportive markets.

Lesson: **redistribution of property can underpin broader economic transformation** — but it requires complementary investments (credit, market access) to be sustainable.

Latin America: mixed outcomes

In Latin America land reform had mixed results. Mexico's post-revolutionary ejido system redistributed land to communities, but the long-term productivity effects varied based on market access and support. In some cases, half-hearted reforms left elites intact or created fragmented plots without investment. In others, reform catalyzed rural development.

Lesson: **design and follow-through matter.** Land reform without market integration, infrastructure, and technical services can fall short.

Contemporary land issues

Land reform is politically explosive and must navigate legal claims, historical injustice, and modern real-estate dynamics. The lesson is careful sequencing: legal frameworks, finance, land titling clarity, and community involvement are essential.

6. Revolutions, Reparations, and Radical Redistribution

Where incremental politics fails, revolutions have sometimes redistributed wealth — with varied and morally fraught outcomes. Revolutions can dismantle oligarchies and nationalize wealth, but they also risk authoritarian capture, violence, and economic dislocation.

Revolutions' high stakes

Revolutions in Russia (1917), China (1949), and elsewhere redistributed land and capital on a massive scale. They also reshaped class structures and, crucially, installed new political orders that often concentrated power rather than diffusing it. Revolutionary redistribution shows that force can break fortifications but also that new rules matter — who writes them and with what constraints.

Lesson: **force can produce rapid redistribution, but without institutions that constrain power and embed rights, gains can be reversed or re-cast as new hierarchies.** This explains the modern progressive preference for democratic and legal channels where possible.

Reparations and restorative justice

Reparative programs — the transfer of resources to victims of historical injustice — are an important but politically contested form of redistribution. Examples vary widely: post-WWII German restitution for victims of the Holocaust; South Africa's complicated debates around land and reparations; and ongoing conversations in settler states about indigenous rights and redress.

Lesson: **reparations confront thorny questions of evidence, political feasibility, and administrative design.** Done well, they acknowledge historical wrongs and redistribute; done poorly, they can be tokenistic or divisive. The design challenge is to make reparative programs substantial, transparent, and forward-looking.

7. International Redistribution: Debt Relief and Aid Reforms

Redistribution is not only national. International flows — debt relief, aid, and global tax policy — matter for global inequality.

Debt relief: breathing room for public investment

Debt overhangs have strangled public spending in many lower-income countries. Debt relief (partial cancellation, restructuring) can free fiscal space for education, health, and climate adaptation. The Heavily Indebted Poor Countries (HIPC) initiative and other programs have mixed records but do show the potential of coordinated international action.

Lesson: **debt relief must be paired with institutional reform and safeguards against future predatory lending** — otherwise structural problems recur.

Aid redesign: grants over loans for vulnerability

When external finance is given as loans, recipient countries may be locked into future repayment and austerity. For climate adaptation and loss & damage, grants are ethically and economically preferable. Mobilizing grant finance — through global institutions or new instruments — is central to equitable global redistribution.

Lesson: **the form of transfers matters.** Grants, technical assistance, and concessional finance designed around domestic agency produce better developmental outcomes than procyclical borrowing.

8. What Worked: Common Threads Across Successes

Looking across history, several common ingredients recur in successful redistribution episodes:

1. **Coalitions, not solo actors.** Labor, civil society, progressive elites, and political parties often had to combine forces. The New Deal and Nordic models rested on cross-class bargains.
2. **Crisis or political opening.** Large redistributions are easier during crises (war, depression) or after structural shocks that undermine status quo legitimacy.
3. **Institutional embedding.** Laws, independent agencies, collective agreements, and constitutional protections turned transient gains into lasting institutions.
4. **Administrative capacity.** Tax collection, regulation, and program delivery require capable states. Without capacity, programs remain symbolic.
5. **Narrative framing.** Successful reforms had powerful stories: collective sacrifice during wartime, the moral case for social insurance, or the economic case for mass consumption.
6. **Enforcement and measurement.** Visible rules with enforcement resources and metrics prevented backsliding.

9. What Went Wrong: Cautions and Reversals

History also provides cautionary tales. Gains can erode.

- **Backlash & political realignment.** Conservative countermobilization (think of the post-1970s neoliberal turn) can roll back redistribution through deregulation, tax cuts, and deunionization.

- **Globalization & capital mobility.** As capital became more mobile, unilateral national measures faced limits — capital flight, tax arbitrage, and offshoring undermined old bargains.

- **Institutional capture.** New institutions can be captured by elites if oversight is weak; social programs can become vehicles for patronage if transparency is absent.

- **Inadequate inclusivity.** Many postwar programs excluded women, racial minorities, and informal workers by design or oversight — locking inequality into the welfare state.

- **Technological and economic change.** Automation and platformization altered labor markets in ways that old bargaining models didn't anticipate.

Lesson: **durability requires constant care.** Institutions must be defended, adapted, and democratized. Administrative funding, anti-capture safeguards, and inclusive policy design are non-negotiable.

10. Translating Lessons to Today's Fight

What does history tell us about prying open today's fortified piñata?

1. **Build broad, pragmatic coalitions.** Bring labor, small businesses hurt by monopoly, public service users, and civic groups together around concrete wins (childcare, living wages, procurement).
2. **Use moments of crisis strategically.** Crises create openings — but insist on inclusive design to avoid repeat exclusions.
3. **Institutionalize gains.** Don't treat a wage increase or a transparency law as the end; embed enforcement funding, monitoring dashboards, and legal protections.
4. **Pair domestic policy with international cooperation.** A national wealth tax is less credible without cross-border transparency and minimum tax frameworks.
5. **Invest in administrative capacity.** Enforcement without resources is a photograph, not a tool.
6. **Center narrative and culture.** Policy succeeds when framed in terms of shared investment and dignity, not mere punishment of success.
7. **Anticipate adaptation.** Seal loopholes, anticipate legal challenges, and design measures that are hard to arbitrage.

11. Final Synthesis: Why the Past Should Inspire Strategy, Not Nostalgia

History gives both encouragement and humility. It proves piñatas can be breached; it also warns that gains are never automatic or permanent. The past shows that redistribution that endures is political, institutional, and cultural work — not only economic engineering.

For modern reformers, the practical takeaway is a design ethic: match ambition with enforcement, combine visible local wins with institutional reform, build coalitions that can defend gains, and link domestic change to international rules where necessary. In short: be systemic, be strategic, be persistent.

Tools of Redistribution — The Sticks

If redistribution is not a prayer but a craft, then this chapter is the workshop. Here we lay out practical implements — the sticks — that open the piñata and let candy flow to more hands. Some sticks are blunt and political (unions, campaign finance reform); some are technical and fiscal (progressive taxation, wealth taxes); some reshape markets (antitrust, corporate governance); and some change ownership (public enterprises, co-ops). Each tool has variants, trade-offs, enforcement needs, and political pathways. This chapter is a catalog and a how-to: what the tool does, why it helps reduce concentrated advantage, how it can be designed and implemented, what to watch out for, and how it fits into a larger strategy.

1 — Progressive Taxation: The Core Stick

What it is. Progressive taxation raises a larger share of public revenue from those with higher incomes (and, optionally, wealth). It can operate through personal income tax (with graduated rates), capital gains taxation, corporate taxes, and redistributive transfers financed by those revenues.

Why it matters. Taxes are the most direct, flexible instrument to reshape after-tax income distribution. Evidence shows that progressive personal income taxes and well-designed tax systems are effective levers to reduce inequality while allowing public investment in health, education, and infrastructure that multiplies opportunity. International institutions emphasize the role progressive taxation plays in reducing inequality and creating fiscal space for social investment.

Design choices and practical variants

- **Graduated PIT rates.** A graduated personal income tax with higher marginal rates at the top increases progressivity. Design choices include number of brackets, top marginal rate, surtaxes, and thresholds indexed to inflation.

- **Capital income parity.** Tax policy can align tax rates on capital income (capital gains, dividends) with earned income, reducing the preferential treatment that concentrates returns among asset owners.

- **Negative income tax / earned income tax credit (EITC).** These tilt support to working households through refundable credits, increasing work incentives while redistributing.

- **Corporate tax design.** Corporate taxes raise revenue directly and can be structured to discourage excessive leverage and profit shifting. Anti-avoidance rules and minimum taxes on multinationals are critical complements.

- **Targeted surtaxes.** Temporary or permanent surtaxes (for example, a modest surcharge above a high threshold) allow flexibility for deficit reduction or funding priorities.

Implementation details and enforcement

- **Base-broadening first.** Reducing exemptions and closing carve-outs often yields more revenue and is fairer than piling on higher rates that are easily gamed. Complexity breeds avoidance; simpler broad bases are harder to arbitrage.

- **Information systems.** Tax authorities need modern information systems to match reported income to bank data, asset registries, and international reports (FATCA/CRS). Information exchange is essential to prevent sheltering.

- **Anti-avoidance legislation.** General anti-abuse rules, controlled foreign company rules, and thin-capitalization rules reduce classic avoidance channels.

- **Administration funding.** Progressive rules require auditors, data analysts, and legal units. Underfunded tax administrations are the soft underbelly of any ambitious tax redesign.

Political strategy

- Emphasize revenue for public goods (education, health), not punishment. Frame as investment in opportunity.

- Use phasing: enact base-broadening first, strengthen enforcement, then adjust rates — that makes changes harder to evade and reduces political backlash.

- Combine transparency with fairness: publish beneficial ownership registries and use automatic information exchange to counter the "they'll just flee" narrative.

Trade-offs and pitfalls

- Tax increases with weak enforcement lead to capital flight and avoidance; counter that with global cooperation and information exchange.

- High corporate rates without anti-avoidance can simply shift incidence. The design matters more than headline rates.

2 — Wealth Taxes and Annual Billionaire Levies: A Direct Approach to Capital Concentration

What it is. Wealth taxation typically imposes an annual tax on net assets above a threshold (with progressive rates for larger fortunes). Variants include one-off levies (temporary), recurrent progressive taxes, and minimum taxation standards on ultra-high net worth individuals.

Why it matters. Income taxes capture flows; wealth taxes capture accumulated stock. Because much of modern inequality is stock-based (assets, real estate, private stakes), wealth taxes directly address entrenched fortunes. Recent research shows a credible wealth tax, well enforced, would raise meaningful revenue and temper extreme concentration. Prominent economists have proposed modest annual rates targeted at the ultra-rich to raise revenue and rebalance long-run distribution.

Design issues

- **Threshold and rates.** Set a high threshold (e.g., \$50m or \$100m) so tax affects the top fraction; progressive bands above thresholds (e.g., 1–3%) limit revenue drag and concentrate burden on largest fortunes.

- **Valuation rules.** Accurate asset valuation is the technical heart: use market valuations for listed assets, standard approaches for real estate and business interests, periodic marking for illiquid assets.

- **Liquidity protections.** To avoid forcing asset sales, exemptions or deferrals (with interest) for family businesses or illiquid holdings can be included, coupled with anti-abuse rules to prevent artificial illiquidity claims.

- **International coordination.** Given mobility of capital, cross-border cooperation, minimum standards, or withholding rules reduce flight risk. Global agreements (or regional ones) make enforcement feasible.

Enforcement and administrative feasibility

- **Beneficial ownership registries** and public disclosure cut the opacity that enables evasion.

- **Reporting requirements** from banks, asset managers, and platforms are essential; automated exchange and CRA-style systems help.

- **Penalties and audits** for misreporting must be credible; the tax must be backed by legal frameworks that discourage avoidance.

Political strategy

- Introduce as targeted, modest-rate taxes on the ultra-top and pair with popular uses (climate resilience, universal childcare, debt reduction).

- Combat narratives of capital flight by demonstrating other countries that keep wealthy residents (Spain's recent experience is illustrative) and by building international minimums. Recent policy debates at multilateral fora show political appetite for coordinated minimum taxation on the ultra-wealthy.

Critiques and responses

- **Administrative complexity.** Yes — but modern data and reporting systems reduce costs; the revenue potential at the top can justify administrative investment.

- **Capital flight.** Mitigate with exit taxes, exchange of information, residency rules, and coordination.

- **Distortion.** Carefully set thresholds and rates minimize impacts on entrepreneurship and small business owners.

3 — Labor Power: Unions and Collective Bargaining

What it is. Strengthening unions and collective bargaining empowers workers to negotiate wages, benefits, and working conditions. Legal frameworks (right to organize, card check, sectoral bargaining) shape union density and effectiveness.

Why it matters. Unionized sectors historically compressed wage distribution, raised middle incomes, and broadened access to benefits (health, pensions). Research estimates of the union wage premium commonly find meaningful effects on wages and inequality reduction. Unions also change firms' norms — from cost-minimizing HR models to negotiated standards — lifting bargaining power across nonunion labor markets as well.

Design levers

- **Legal protection for organizing.** Strong penalties for employer interference, quick remedial procedures, and real remedies (e.g., reinstatement + damages) deter union-busting.

- **Card-check or majority recognition.** Reduce procedural burdens for certification.

- **Sectoral bargaining and industry councils.** Wage floors set by sector prevent a race to the bottom in fragmented markets.

- **Collective bargaining for new sectors.** Update laws to cover gig workers, platform drivers, and independent contractors in ways that preserve bargaining power.

- **Co-management and worker voice.** Board-level representation, works councils, or statutory consultation rights give workers institutional influence over governance in addition to wages.

Implementation and sequencing

- Start with low-cost fixes that build power (stronger penalties for unfair labor practices), then phase in structural changes (sectoral bargaining, board representation).

- Pair union strengthening with active labor policies: retraining, portability of benefits, and public supports for transitions.

Political strategy

- Build cross-class coalitions: small-business owners worried about monopsony, consumers harmed by stagnation, and younger workers seeking career ladders.
- Highlight win-win cases where sectoral bargaining stabilized supply and improved product quality (construction, ports).

Caveats

- Overly rigid bargaining in some contexts can reduce firm flexibility; surviving models balance negotiated floors with firm-level adaptability.
- Union revitalization often requires cultural and organizational rebuilding; legal change alone is necessary but not sufficient.

4 — Antitrust, Competition Policy, and Corporate Accountability

What it is. Antitrust enforcement, merger review, and rules limiting market concentration protect competition, prevent rent extraction, and preserve dynamism. Corporate accountability includes rules on executive pay, disclosure, and fiduciary duties that shape corporate behavior.

Why it matters. Market concentration reduces worker bargaining power, raises prices, lowers innovation incentives in some sectors, and allows rent extraction. Stronger antitrust enforcement that blocks anti-competitive mergers or breaks up dominant firms has measurable effects on prices and market structure. Empirical work shows that tougher merger screens can reduce price increases and restore competition. Recent high-profile merger interventions (and some judicial blocks) illustrate the practical power of enforcement.

Policy levers

- **Harden merger standards.** Use broader metrics (labor market effects, innovation, consumer choice) rather than narrow short-term price screens.

- **Vertical and killer acquisitions.** Review acquisitions that eliminate nascent competitors or create gatekeeping power.

- **Platform regulation.** Address data monopolies, self-preferencing, and interoperability to reduce network-effect lock-in.

- **Limit shareholder primacy.** Encourage or require corporations to consider workers and communities (stakeholder governance), or strengthen fiduciary duties to reflect long-term value.

- **Executive pay controls and clawbacks.** Tighten rules around pay disclosure, say-on-pay, and clawbacks for misconduct.

Enforcement capacity

- Fund competition authorities properly; hire sectoral experts (tech, pharmaceuticals), and give them investigatory tools (data access, rapid injunctions).

- Create special units to review serial acquirers (platforms that buy startups to neutralize competition).

Political strategy

- Frame antitrust as consumer and worker protection: lower prices, better choices, and higher wages in competitive labor markets.

- Partner with state attorneys general and international counterparts for multi-jurisdictional enforcement.

Trade-offs

- Overzealous intervention can chill legitimate scale economies; well-calibrated tests and empirical analysis are crucial.

- Antitrust is a long game — courts and standards matter. Political appointments to agencies make a difference; institutional independence helps.

5 — Public Ownership, Municipal Enterprises, and Cooperatives

What it is. Public ownership refers to government-owned entities providing utilities, transport, housing, or other public goods. Cooperatives and worker-owned firms democratize ownership and retain surplus within communities and workers rather than distributing it to distant shareholders.

Why it matters. In sectors characterized by natural monopolies (water, transit), public ownership can prioritize access, affordability, and long-term infrastructure over short-term profit. Cooperatives retain value in communities, generate more equitable compensation structures, and can stabilize local economies. Mondragón and municipal utilities offer practical models of scaled worker ownership and public enterprise.

Design options

- **Municipal utilities and public banks.** Cities run energy, water, broadband, and public banks to direct lending to local priorities and keep returns public.

- **Public-private hybrids.** Social enterprises or public benefit corporations combine performance incentives with public accountability.

- **Worker cooperatives.** Support through financing, technical assistance, cooperative banks, and legal forms that make conversions feasible.

- **Community land trusts (CLTs).** Land held in trust for affordable housing reduces speculative pressure and preserves affordability.

Practical mechanisms

- **Seed capital and public financing.** Low-interest loans, public procurement preference, and incubation programs help co-ops scale.

- **Legal frameworks.** Facilitate worker buyouts with tax incentives, cooperative ownership laws, and favorable pension arrangements.

- **Governance safeguards.** Ensure public enterprises have transparent governance, public reporting, and clear mandates to avoid capture.

Political strategy

- Start with targeted pilots: municipal broadband, public housing co-ops, or worker buyouts of distressed plants. Demonstrated success builds legitimacy.

- Use procurement rules to create demand (buy from co-ops and local public providers).

Pitfalls

- Public enterprises can suffer from politicization and inefficiency if governance is weak. Transparency and professional management are required.

- Co-ops need supportive ecosystems: finance, training, and market access.

6 — Universal Basic Income (UBI) and Targeted Transfers

What it is. UBI is an unconditional cash payment to individuals (flat, universal) that provides a floor of security. Variants include guaranteed minimum income, negative income tax, and targeted basic income for specific populations.

Why it matters. Direct cash transfers can reduce poverty, improve mental health, and enable risk-taking. Pilots (e.g., GiveDirectly in Kenya, Finland's experiment) show meaningful welfare gains and improvements in security; the evidence on employment effects is mixed but generally indicates no large negative labor supply impacts and some positive effects on wellbeing.

Design choices

- **Universal vs. targeted.** Universal programs reduce stigma and administrative complexity but cost more; targeted programs are cheaper but require means testing.

- **Regularity and size.** Monthly predictable payments strengthen planning; lump sums can boost investment in assets but may have different long-term effects.

- **Complementary services.** Pair transfers with access to health care, childcare, and training to maximize long-term returns.

Implementation notes

- **Pilot scale and context matter.** Results from low-income countries and short pilots don't automatically translate to high-income economies; careful pilot design matters.

- **Fiscal realism.** Financing via progressive taxation or re-allocating specific subsidies must be explicit; avoid underfunded symbolic promises.

Political strategy

- Frame pilots as insurance and productivity enhancers (support entrepreneurship, caregiving).

- Highlight real-world benefits (reduced stress, better health outcomes) to build a coalition across voters.

Pitfalls

- Poorly funded universal promises create fiscal stress.

- Political opponents can frame UBI as reducing work ethic; evidence shows nuanced effects that must be communicated clearly.

7 — Campaign Finance Reform and Democratic Defense

What it is. Reforms that limit the ability of wealthy actors to buy political influence — public financing, small-donor matching, disclosure rules, limits on dark money — reshape who sets the rules.

Why it matters. Money translates into access and agenda control. Public matching funds for small donors, for example, amplify ordinary voices and reduce dependence on big donors. Evidence from city programs and research finds that matching programs diversify candidate pools and reduce elite influence.

Tool variants

- **Small-donor matching (e.g., $6:$1).** Amplifies grassroots contributions dramatically.

- **Public seed grants + matching.** Enable challengers to compete early.

- **Full public financing.** Provide candidates with a fixed public pot if they meet small-donor thresholds and ethics rules.

- **Disclosure and dark-money limits.** Tighten disclosure of political expenditures, including so-called independent expenditures.

Implementation

- **Robust verification.** Fraud prevention, contribution limits enforcement, and easy public access to data.

- **Match targeting.** Consider higher matching for small donations to increase equity (e.g., higher match for first $200 of contributions).

- **Civic education tie-ins.** Encourage voter engagement so the matched donors reflect active constituents.

Political strategy

- Frame reforms as anti-corruption and pro-accountability.

- Pilot at municipal/state level to build evidence and scale up.

Pitfalls

- Legal constraints (Supreme Court decisions or constitutional protections) can limit some reforms; design must align with judicial frameworks.

- Matches require budgets; show return on investment via cleaner governance and more representative policies.

8 — Legal Enforcement, Transparency, and Anti-Corruption

What it is. Laws are paper without enforcement. Transparency (beneficial ownership registries, disclosure rules) plus strong enforcement capacities (tax investigators, anti-fraud units, empowered regulators) close gaps where wealth flows out of the public eye.

Why it matters. Information is the foundation of modern enforcement. International frameworks like automatic exchange of information (CRS), FATCA, and mutual legal assistance have reduced some offshore hiding; continued development of reporting standards and enforcement reduces avoidance opportunities.

Practical elements

- **Beneficial ownership registries.** Public or accessible registries reveal who ultimately controls corporations and trusts.

- **Automatic information exchange.** Strengthen cross-border data flows and cooperation on audits.

- **Special enforcement units.** Dedicated financial crimes units, asset recovery teams, and criminal enforcement deter sophisticated evasion.

- **Whistleblower protections and incentives.** Encourage insiders to report fraud with legal and financial safeguards.

Implementation

- Phase in disclosure with support for developing country administrations.

- Provide technical assistance and capacity building for tax authorities and anti-corruption prosecutors.

Political strategy

- Tie transparency to popular outcomes: more revenue for schools and hospitals.

- Use investigative journalism and public reporting to mobilize opinion and political cover for enforcement funding.

Pitfalls

- Secrecy jurisdictions resist transparency; international pressure and sanctions may be necessary.

- Privacy concerns must be balanced with public interest; narrow exceptions can be provided for personal safety.

9 — Complementary Tools: Procurement, Zoning, and Public Investment

Redistribution isn't only about taxes and transfers. Public procurement, land policy, and targeted investment steer markets.

- **Progressive procurement**: Use public buying power to favor local suppliers, co-ops, and firms that meet labor and environmental standards; direct demand to firms that share prosperity.

- **Zoning for inclusion**: Reform land-use rules to expand affordable housing near jobs and transit; use inclusionary zoning and community land trusts.

- **Public investment**: Invest in early childhood, broadband, transit, and R&D — all yield high social returns and equalize opportunity.

These measures carry immediate local benefits and create the conditions that make other sticks more effective.

10 — Sequencing and Strategy: How to Use the Sticks Together

No single tool wins. The sticks are most effective in bundles and in sequence.

A pragmatic sequence:

1. **Transparency & enforcement start.** Publish ownership registries; fund tax admin; sign automatic exchange agreements. These reduce evasion and make later tax reforms credible.

2. **Targeted redistribution wins.** Increase EITC and child benefits to build public support with visible gains.
3. **Labor & competition law reforms.** Strengthen bargaining rights and antitrust enforcement to rebalance power in markets.
4. **Progressive taxation & wealth measures.** With better information and enforcement, raise revenues progressively and (where politically feasible) introduce wealth levies on the top.
5. **Public investment & ownership tools.** Use new revenue to scale childcare, housing, public banks, and co-op financing.
6. **Democratic reforms.** Solidify campaign finance and disclosure rules to keep the policy environment responsive to broad interests.

Why sequencing matters. Tightening reporting and enforcement before raising rates reduces avoidance. Building visible wins (child benefits, wage gains via unions) creates political coalitions supportive of deeper reforms.

11 — Measuring Success: Metrics That Matter

To know if a stick is working, track the right metrics:

- **Distributional outcomes.** Post-tax, post-transfer Gini; share of national wealth held by top 1%/0.1%.

- **Labor metrics.** Median wages, union density, bargaining coverage.

- **Market metrics.** Herfindahl-Hirschman Index in key sectors; markups and profit shares.

- **Fiscal metrics.** Revenue as % GDP from progressive taxes; tax gap estimates.

- **Access indicators.** Childcare coverage, housing affordability, broadband access, enrollment rates.

Good measurement allows course corrections and defends reforms against capture and erosion.

12 — Political Economics: Building Coalitions to Defend the Sticks

Technical design matters, but politics runs the show. Winning and defending sticks requires:

- **Broad coalitions.** Workers, small businesses that suffer from monopolies, public-service recipients, and civic organizations.

- **Narrative work.** Frame reforms as investments in shared capacity (schools, transit, health) rather than moral crusades. Emphasize fairness and reciprocity.

- **Institutional anchors.** Create statutory protections for enforcement budgets; public participation in rulemaking; and legal standards that make rollback costly.

- **International diplomacy.** Tax and wealth issues require multilateral coordination; build alliances with like-minded countries.

13 — Common Objections & Quick Replies

- **"Taxes kill growth."** Evidence shows moderate progressive taxation, paired with smart public investment, need not impair aggregate growth — and can enhance long-run productivity by funding education, health, and infrastructure.

- **"Wealth taxes are impractical."** They are administratively demanding — but for the ultra-rich, transparency and international cooperation make annual levies feasible; place them in a package with stronger enforcement.

- **"Unions are outdated."** Modernized rules for organizing in the gig economy and sectoral bargaining can revive worker voice in ways that fit contemporary labor markets.

- **"Antitrust will harm innovation."** Well-crafted enforcement targets exclusionary and rent-extracting conduct; dynamic innovation can coexist with competition policy that prevents gatekeeping.

14 — A Short Playbook: First 100 Days (Example)

If a government wanted to credibly start breaking a fortified piñata, an initial program might include:

1. **Transparency executive orders**: beneficial-ownership registries and open public procurement lists. (Immediate visibility.)
2. **Budget boost for tax admin**: hire auditors, deploy data analytics teams. (Makes enforcement credible.)
3. **Small visible transfers**: expand child benefits or EITC to show concrete gains. (Builds public buy-in.)
4. **Labor protections**: strengthen penalties for union-busting and expedite certification. (Empowers workers.)
5. **Antitrust review**: pause large mergers pending modernized guidelines. (Signals seriousness.)
6. **Campaign finance pilot**: small-donor matching for municipal races. (Reduces dependence on big donors.)

These moves are politically achievable, build momentum, and block quick accommodation by entrenched interests.

15 — The Craftsman's Mindset

Tools matter; design matters more. A stick is more than its material — it is how you shape, brace, and swing it. Redistribution succeeds when policy is designed with enforcement, sequencing, coalition building, and measurement in view. The sticks in this chapter are not theoretical abstractions; they are practical instruments that, properly crafted and used together, can open the piñata and put the candy into hands that have too long been empty.

Overcoming Resistance: The Counterattack

If redistribution is the art of opening a stubborn piñata, then expect that the people who built the fortifications will fight to keep it closed. They have tools, tactics, resources, and time on their side; they also understand how to exploit institutional weaknesses, social narratives, and legal systems to blunt change. This chapter maps the most common defensive playbook — propaganda and narrative warfare, organized lobbying and capture, legal strategies (including strategic lawsuits and judicial capture), financial pressure and campaign influence, and physical repression — and then lays out how movements, reformers, and publics can preempt, blunt, or neutralize those counterattacks.

This is a tactical manual and a strategic argument. Knowing the enemy's playbook is not a cynical celebration of conflict; it is a prerequisite for designing measures that last. Every defensive tactic has a counter. Narrative warfare can be answered with strategic framing and storytelling. Lobbying and capture can be met by transparency, enforcement, and public mobilization. SLAPPs and litigation can be met by legal-defense networks and anti-SLAPP laws. Repression can be met by documenting abuses, widening international pressure, and ensuring legal accountability. The point is straightforward: to break a fortified piñata you do more than swing hard — you anticipate who will tug the rope and where they will hide the ladder.

Part I — What Elites Actually Do: The Defensive Playbook

Movements often assume resistance will take the form of reasoned policy debate. Sometimes it does. Far more often, resistance uses a mixed set of techniques designed to delay, deflect, delegitimize, or criminalize reform.

1. Propaganda, PR, and Narrative Warfare

What it looks like. Sophisticated public-relations campaigns designed to shape public opinion and reframe reform as risky, unfair, or economically harmful. This ranges from commission-funded research and op-eds to paid social-media influencers, astroturf campaigns (fake grassroots), and well-funded advertising blitzes. The modern PR ecosystem is fast, targeted, and able to weaponize fragmentary truths: a small technical risk becomes an existential threat in 30-second ad spots.

How it works. Messages that align with existing heuristics stick. People respond to simple frames: "Jobs versus taxes," "freedom versus coercion," "innovation versus regulation." A PR campaign that repeatedly pairs a proposed reform with a frightening story (jobs lost, businesses closing) will change how citizens instinctively react — even in the face of complex evidence to the contrary. Funds underwrite message testing, micro-targeting, and rapid-response infrastructure that is hard for underfunded movements to match.

Why it's effective. The combination of money and media slows reform by shifting public opinion and shaping the terms of parliamentary and electoral debate. A powerful advertising wave gives politicians cover to oppose or dilute reforms; it also provides talking points for sympathetic commentators, experts, and think tanks.

Illustrative mechanics in the real world. In recent election cycles and policy fights, shadowy pools of funding have been used to underwrite coordinated amplification and to obscure donors' identities, multiplying the effect of message campaigns and protecting the sources from accountability. Initiatives that seem like spontaneous civic concern are sometimes manufactured behind the scenes to serve narrow interests.

2. Lobbying, Revolving Doors, and Institutional Capture

What it looks like. Corporations and wealthy actors hire lobbyists, fund research, draft model legislation, and cultivate relationships with regulatory agencies. They recruit former regulators and lawmakers into their ranks — and sometimes hire the reverse: sending their people into government roles. The result is a flow of personnel and ideas that aligns public institutions with private interests.

How it works. Access begets influence. Lobbyists translate technical preferences into legal text and sit through rule-writing sessions; they testify in hearings, contribute to campaign coffers, and provide testimony and "expert" reports. The revolving door — staff who move between industry and regulatory bodies — deepens these ties. Empirical evidence shows that movement between public agencies and the industries they oversee is widespread and correlated in many cases with softer enforcement or more industry-friendly outcomes.

Why it's effective. Lobbying is not merely persuasion; it is institutional muscle. Well-funded actors can sustain long-term campaigns across legislatures, bureaucracies, and courts, while social movements often rely on episodic bursts of attention. Over time, the institutional preferences shaped by continual lobbying harden into path dependencies that protect the status quo.

3. Legal Strategies: Litigation, SLAPPs, and Judicial Capture

What it looks like. Strategic litigation is a double-edged sword: movements use courts to protect rights; elites use them to block reforms or intimidate critics. Two broad legal tactics are particularly common:

- **Defensive litigation and delay.** Corporations sue to slow regulatory rollouts, obtain injunctions, or force resource-draining discovery processes. Courts can become arenas where reform is strangled by time and expense.

- **Strategic Lawsuits Against Public Participation (SLAPPs).** Powerful actors bring suits not primarily to win on the law, but to impose legal costs on critics — journalists, community groups, and activists — with the aim of chilling speech and discouraging mobilization. SLAPPs can bankrupt small groups and turn public attention toward procedural battles rather than substantive change. Reports and case studies show the growing use of SLAPPs against environmental defenders, journalists, and community activists.

Judicial capture. Appointments, political influence on courts, and forum-shopping for sympathetic judges combine to make litigation an arena where political outcomes are increasingly contested. In some contexts, litigants seek advantageous jurisdictions or delay tactics designed explicitly to wait out political cycles.

Why it's effective. The legal system offers tools of attrition. Even when movements ultimately prevail, the costs — financial, emotional, organizational — can be crippling and can divert energy away from mobilization and coalition building.

4. Dark Money, Campaign Finance, and Political Pressure

What it looks like. Wealth buys attention: donations to candidates, funding for political parties' shadow apparatus, and limitless spending from groups that can hide donors' identities. "Dark money" floods advertising markets and funds message infrastructure that protects favored policies and politicians.

How it works. With legal loopholes and judicial decisions enabling unrestricted third-party spending, concentrated wealth acts as a continuous amplifier for policy preferences. The result is a politics more responsive to concentrated money than dispersed citizens.

Why it's effective. Money buys time: incumbents who rely on wealthy donors resist reforms that threaten donor interests. More than that, money funds the informational ecosystem described above — think tanks, loyal journalists, and targeted outreach — making counter-mobilization harder for movements that rely on grassroots funding.

5. Repression: Policing, Criminalization, and Administrative Sanctions

What it looks like. In moments of high conflict, states (sometimes at the urging of private actors) use policing strategies, administrative sanctions, and even emergency powers to suppress dissent. Tactics include mass arrests, kettling, use of force, criminal charges, restrictive permitting regimes, and aggressive civil enforcement (fines, asset freezes).

How it works. Beyond physical suppression, legalistic tools — anti-protest laws, expanded definitions of public-order offenses, and the use of criminal or civil liability against organizers — create chilling effects. Human-rights organizations have documented these tactics across democracies and more repressive states alike: excessive use of force, misuse of public-order laws, and legal tools crafted to preempt protests.

Why it's effective. Repression is the ultimate dampener on collective action: it raises the personal stakes of visible protest, deters participation, and sends messages about risk. Even when abuses are temporary or illegal, the fear they generate persists.

6. Co-Optation: Philanthropy, Partnerships, and Partial Concessions

What it looks like. Corporations and wealthy philanthropists fund initiatives that look like reform — pilot programs, advisory boards, social-impact partnerships — that also channel agenda-setting and narrative control. They may offer targeted assistance (scholarships, programs) that calms critics while leaving broader structural drivers intact.

How it works. Co-optation blunts critique by offering limited goods under private control. It buys legitimacy, creates insiders, and produces case studies that can be cited to argue broader reforms are unnecessary. Philanthropic funding is especially effective because it can underwrite the creation of institutions (think tanks, research centers, cultural institutions) that shape long-term discourse.

Why it's effective. When critique becomes negotiation, movement energy diffuses into design consultations rather than structural change. Co-optation converts potential opponents into collaborators who often argue for incrementalism rather than systemic redesign.

Part II — How Movements Can Preempt, Counter, and Neutralize the Counterattack

Mapping the turn-of-the-century defensive playbook is only useful if each tactic has a counter. Below are practical, evidence-informed strategies that successful movements and reformers use to survive and win.

1. Preempt with Narrative: Own the Frame Before They Do

Principle. Messages win before laws do. If reformers do not control the frame, opponents will define the debate as a battle over scary hypotheticals rather than concrete returns.

Tactics.

- **Frame early and simply.** Use values-based language (security, fairness, shared prosperity) and concrete stories (people who get early-childhood care because of a program, small-business owners who benefit from a living wage) rather than abstract policy talk. The marriage-equality movement and some economic campaigns demonstrate how storytelling shifts public opinion by humanizing issues and making them relatable.

- **Test and iterate.** Use polling and small tests (A/B message testing, digital experiments) to find resonance before national rollouts.

- **Outproduce on media.** Match message cadence: rapid responses to opponent attacks, steadier drip of stories about reform beneficiaries, and durable content (long-form pieces, investigative reports) that supply journalists with material.

- **Audience segmentation.** Tailor frames for different constituencies: small-business owners worry about different trade-offs than urban mothers; speak directly to their values and interests.

Why this works. Narrative work prevents opponents from defining the reform as reckless. It builds the scaffolding of consent that makes legal and political change less risky for elected officials.

2. Build Legal Defenses Before You Need Them

Principle. Litigation is a weapon for both sides — movements should prepare legal shields before opponents swing.

Tactics.

- **Legal defense funds.** Establish pooled funds (city, national, or sectoral) for bail, legal fees, and counsel. Organizations like the National Lawyers Guild and other movement legal structures have long-run experience providing mass-defense and strategic litigation support. These funds lower the personal cost of participation and help neutralize SLAPP-style intimidation tactics.

- **Pro bono networks and rapid-response councils.** Build rosters of lawyers who can mobilize quickly for arrests, injunctions, or civil suits.

- **Anti-SLAPP legislation advocacy.** Push for strong anti-SLAPP laws that allow quick dismissal of frivolous suits and reimbursement of legal costs for defendants. Where anti-SLAPP protections exist, they can blunt the strategic impact of intimidation litigation.

- **Strategic litigation offensively.** Use the courts to set precedents that protect protest rights, clarify regulatory authority, and break oligopolistic power. Targeted, well-chosen cases can create durable legal protections.

Why this works. Legal defense capacity transforms litigation from a weapon of attrition into a neutral arena. It raises the cost for elite actors who would weaponize courts and preserves movement momentum.

3. Transparency and the Public Ledger: Make the Defensive Moves Visible

Principle. Secrecy is a force multiplier for elites; transparency undermines it.

Tactics.

- **Publish money flows.** Campaign to require disclosure of donors, beneficial ownership of entities, and corporate political spending. Public registers and investigative journalism can expose influence networks and change the incentives for secret spending. Evidence shows dark-money expenditures shape agendas; disclosure reduces their opacity.

- **Track lobbying and personnel flows.** Maintain public databases of revolving-door hires, lobbyist meetings, and advisory relationships. Naming and documenting creates reputational pressure and furnishes journalists with leads.

- **Open data and FOIA pressure.** Use Freedom of Information tools to document regulatory meetings and unrecorded influence.

Why this works. Visibility makes capture harder. When a politician knows a meeting will be publicized, they are less likely to make shadow deals; when corporate donations must be disclosed, reputational costs increase.

4. Institutionalize Coalitions: Effective Alliances Are Diverse and Durable

Principle. Durable reform requires durable coalitions that cut across identities and interests — not only traditional left-right coalitions but also groups that can act as policy anchors.

Tactics.

- **Cross-class alliances.** Bring small-business owners, consumer groups, and public-interest advocates into coalitions. For example, local small firms often suffer from monopolistic suppliers; antitrust reforms can be framed as helping both workers and small businesses.

- **Municipal and regional networks.** Cities can be laboratories: winning reforms in a cluster of cities builds national plausibility and forces national debate. Urban victories (minimum wages, public housing co-ops, municipal broadband) have historically catalyzed broader change.

- **Durable institutional partners.** Partner with universities, public-interest law centers, and unions that can provide research, legal support, and organizing infrastructure.

Why this works. Broader coalitions raise the political cost of opposition and increase the set of resources available to defend reforms.

5. Internationalize the Fight: Leverage Cross-Border Mechanisms

Principle. Many defensive tactics exploit jurisdictional boundaries — tax shelters, transnational money, and regulatory arbitrage. International cooperation can blunt these strategies.

Tactics.

- **Push for harmonized transparency rules.** Support and pressure for global standards (automatic exchange of information, beneficial-ownership registries, minimum tax agreements) that make hiding wealth and money harder. Research shows international standards like the Common Reporting Standard (CRS) reduce some cross-border hiding but also reveal coverage gaps that advocacy can exploit.

- **Multilateral litigation strategies.** Use international bodies, like regional human-rights courts or UN mechanisms, to document repression and mobilize international pressure.

- **Transnational networks.** Build connections between NGOs, unions, and civic groups across borders to share tactics and coordinate campaigns against multinational firms.

Why this works. If capital can move globally, so can accountability. International pressure raises reputational and regulatory costs for evasive actors.

6. Harden Institutions: Design for Enforcement and Durability

Principle. Good laws must be matched with institutions that can enforce them. Otherwise, reforms become pageantry.

Tactics.

- **Secure funding streams for enforcement.** Change budget rules so agencies have stable funding that isn't easily starved. Institutional independence — from appointments to budgets — reduces capture risk.

- **Technical assistance and capacity building.** Invest in data systems, auditing experts, and cross-training so that agencies can detect evasion and act.

- **Sunset-review design.** When sunset clauses are politically necessary, pair them with automatic evaluation metrics and renewal thresholds that make rollbacks politically costly.

- **Public-interest rulemaking.** Create participatory rulemaking processes that institutionalize public input and require transparency about industry participation.

Why this works. Laws with teeth are less likely to be gamed. Institutional design is the difference between a regulation that shapes behavior and one that becomes an optional cost of doing business.

7. Defensive Organizing: Protect People, Maintain Momentum

Principle. Movement durability depends on the ability to protect participants and sustain action even under pressure.

Tactics.

- **Training and legal literacy.** Teach participants about rights, de-escalation, and legal procedures. Well-prepared protesters are harder to criminalize and easier to defend.

- **Safety infrastructure.** Establish bail funds, medical teams, and rapid-response hotlines. These reduce the personal cost of involvement and maintain public sympathy.

- **Digital security.** Protect communications from surveillance and legal discovery; teach secure practices that limit opportunistic evidence-gathering against organizers.

- **Narrative resilience.** Develop long-term media strategies that keep stories about participants' dignity, needs, and goals in public view, countering criminalizing frames.

Why this works. Movements that protect participants can maintain higher participation rates and present a more credible political force.

8. Use Litigation Strategically: Offense Is Also Defense

Principle. Courts can be ally and battleground. Smart strategic litigation can lock in wins and create legal roadblocks to rollback.

Tactics.

- **Precedent-building lawsuits.** Target high-impact cases that can create durable legal protections (e.g., for voting rights, protest rights, or labor protections).

- **Coordinate multi-jurisdiction litigation.** Parallel litigation across states or countries creates deterrence and slows opponent adaptation.

- **Amplitude of suits.** Combine individual constitutional claims with aggregated public-interest suits to multiply pressure.

Why this works. Strategic litigation raises the political cost of rollback and creates legal insulation for reforms.

Part III — Case Studies and Tactical Synthesis

It helps to see these tactics in real-world interplay. Below are two short, composite case studies showing how elites deploy counterattacks and how movements counter them.

Case Study A: Raising the Local Minimum Wage

Elite defense. Business groups run advertising claiming job losses, finance media research reports predicting doom, lobby city council members, and threaten to stop local investments. They quietly fund PR groups and think tanks to produce reports over time.

Movement counter. The campaign frames the increase as "public investment in workers and local economies," uses worker stories, builds alliances with small independent businesses that benefit, supplies data on local wage increases and consumer spending, mobilizes a small-donor match and local unions to fund legal defense, and uses rapid response to correct false claims. When companies sued, the movement had prearranged legal help and publicized court filings to show arguments were speculative. Over time, the broad coalition neutralized the scare frame and sustained political pressure until the measure passed and became politically normalized (and difficult to rescind).

Fight-for-$15-style campaigns show how sustained local organizing, legal preparation, and narrative work led to myriad municipal and state wins that collectively shifted national debates.

Case Study B: Preventing a Corporate Hostile Takeover That Threatens Jobs

Elite defense. The acquiring firm hires PR to claim economies of scale, funds lobbying to relax merger review, and quietly files for judicial review to speed approval. It also circulates briefings suggesting the target company will fold without the buyout.

Movement counter. Unions and community groups mobilize a public campaign demanding job protections, commission independent analyses showing market harm, organize public hearings, push state attorneys general to file suit, and coordinate with federal competition authorities. They also highlight the acquiring firm's record of asset-stripping, deploy patient capital proposals for alternative ownership (worker co-op buyout), and secure international attention because the firm depends on foreign reputational capital.

The result can be a negotiated settlement that preserves jobs and enforces antitrust safeguards, or a legal defeat for the acquirer. The key is fusion of legal strategy, coalition pressure, and alternative proposals that make the status quo defensible and the takeover costly.

Part IV — Practical Playbook: What to Build, Now

If you are building a movement or designing policy defense, here's a prioritized checklist — a tactical starter kit that reflects the strategies described above.

1. **Narrative infrastructure.** Invest in message development, storytelling campaigns, and media relationships. Test frames on target audiences before major pushes.
2. **Legal defense and anti-SLAPP measures.** Set up legal funds, secure pro-bono networks, and campaign for anti-SLAPP statutes and speedy dismissal rules.
3. **Transparency campaigns.** Push disclosure laws for money in politics, beneficial ownership, and lobbying; develop public databases and partner with investigative journalists.
4. **Coalition architecture.** Map and cultivate allies across sectors: labor, small business, faith communities, universities, and local governments.
5. **Enforcement-first policy design.** Draft laws with enforcement budgets, clear reporting requirements, and anti-avoidance provisions.
6. **International coordination.** Collaborate with transnational NGOs to expose cross-border avoidance and mobilize reputational pressure.
7. **Protection services.** Build bail funds, rapid legal hotlines, medic teams, and digital-security resources for organizers.
8. **Monitoring and evaluation.** Track opponents'

moves, legal filings, and public sentiment; adapt quickly based on intelligence.

Part V — A Final Political Strategy: Patience, Credibility, and Reciprocity

Breaking fortified systems is neither a sprint nor a purely confrontational exercise. It requires patience, credibility, and an abiding sense of reciprocity.

- **Patience.** Many reforms are multi-year projects. Build institutions and funding that last beyond cycles of attention.

- **Credibility.** Use evidence-based arguments and transparent tactics. Credibility with the public and courts is an asset that neutralizes elite claims of "radicalism" or "recklessness."

- **Reciprocity.** Build reforms that offer real, visible returns to constituencies so support deepens over time. When people see better schools, cleaner transit, higher wages, or new local ownership, the political base for reform solidifies.

Every defensive tactic elites deploy has a counter — sometimes a legal counter, sometimes a narrative one, and often an organizational one. The toolbox in this chapter is about anticipating the counterattack and designing durable defenses and counteroffensives that protect people, sustain momentum, and move institutional power.

Strategy Is Not Only About Winning Laws — It's About Changing the Game

Reformers who imagine that winning a single vote in a legislature is the end of struggle misunderstand the scale of change required to reshape distributional outcomes. The fortified piñata was built over decades; it will not come down from a single swing. To prevail, movements must prepare for the full suite of counterattacks: messaging and money, law and litigation, secrecy and force. The good news is that these defenses are human constructs — they can be exposed, named, and neutralized.

The First Swing — Practical Policy Steps

If the book so far has been diagnosis and strategy, this chapter is the toolbox in your hands. You know the piñata is fortified; you know the sticks. Now we take the first swing — not a fairy-tale instant victory but a set of practical, politically realistic moves that actually change people's lives. These are the policies you can pass or fight for that produce visible returns, build durable coalitions, and create momentum for deeper change. They are deliberately pragmatic: designed to be adoptable in real-world politics, to anticipate counterattacks, and to be sequenced so each step reinforces the next.

This chapter lays out concrete first moves: raising the minimum wage, closing tax loopholes, implementing higher marginal rates on top incomes, expanding public services (healthcare, education, housing), and using public procurement to favor equitable practices. For each measure I cover: what it is, why it works, design choices (the technical nuts and bolts), likely objections and internal responses, enforcement needs, political tactics to pass it, sequencing relative to other reforms, and metrics you should use to know whether it's working.

These are not commandments; they are a playbook. Use them together, not one by one, and adapt the specifics to local legal contexts. The point is less to prescribe exact rates or dollar amounts than to show how to craft policies that are effective, defendable, and politically viable.

Overarching principles for the first swing

Before diving into each policy, a handful of cross-cutting principles will keep you pragmatic and strategic:

1. **Start where people feel the impact.** Early, visible wins (higher wages, lower out-of-pocket costs) create buy-in for deeper changes. People who see tangible improvement are likelier to defend reforms later.
2. **Pair revenue with relief.** Combine tax fixes and higher-rate options with concrete expansions of public services. That linkage — "we're asking more of the wealthy to pay for child care, health care, and housing" — is politically compelling.
3. **Sequence to close escape routes.** Build transparency and enforcement before you raise large rates. Close loopholes and beef up tax administration so avoidance is harder.
4. **Bundle complementary reforms.** Labor strengthening, antitrust, and procurement reforms amplify the effects of wage and tax changes.
5. **Design for enforceability.** A law without an agency is a photo op. Budget enforcement capacity and make legal rules clear to limit gaming.
6. **Build cross-cutting coalitions.** Workers, small-business owners (who often support higher minimum wages), civic groups, health-care advocates, and municipal leaders form a resilient coalition.

7. **Tell the story.** Frame measures as investments in shared security and productivity, not punishment. Emphasize reciprocity: those best able to pay do so to make a functioning society for everyone.

Now we unpack each major first-move policy.

1. Raise the minimum wage (and strengthen basic labor standards)

Why start here

Raising the minimum wage is politically potent because it helps millions of working households immediately. It's easy to understand, easy to explain, and politically attractive across class lines when framed as restoring fairness for jobs that can't be automated away. Higher wages also stimulate local demand, reduce turnover costs, and raise productivity via improved morale and lower absenteeism. For movement politics, wage wins are rallying points — visible, local, and scalable.

Design choices

- **Level and phase-in.** Target a wage that is meaningful relative to living costs — e.g., a regional living wage or a national floor that reflects local cost-of-living differentials. Phase-in over 12–36 months so businesses can adapt.

- **Indexation.** Tie the wage to a transparent metric (median wage, CPI, or a Living Wage Index) to prevent erosion and depoliticize periodic increases.

- **Coverage.** Ensure coverage includes tipped workers, gig workers, and employers who use subcontractors. Use broad legal definitions of "employee" to limit misclassification.

- **Exemptions.** Minimize exemptions. Where transitional relief is necessary (e.g., for very small firms), make it temporary and tied to clear thresholds.

- **Enforcement.** Fund labor-inspection agencies, create easy reporting mechanisms (hotlines and web forms), and establish strong penalties and back-pay remedies for violations.

Complementary measures

- **Schedule fairness rules.** Require advance notice for schedules and compensation for last-minute cancellations.

- **Portable benefits.** For nonstandard workers, implement systems to pool benefits (retirement, paid leave) across gig platforms.

- **Training subsidies.** Pair wage increases with targeted training to raise skills and reduce costs on small employers.

Anticipating objections & counterarguments

- **Objection: job loss.** Evidence shows modest, well-designed increases tend not to cause large employment declines; many employers absorb higher wages through reduced turnover, small price increases, and productivity gains. Frame the wage hike as an investment in local economies (higher spending, reduced reliance on public assistance).

- **Objection: hurts small businesses.** Offer targeted transitional assistance (tax credits, payroll tax holidays for small firms) while maintaining a hard floor so the political defense is not "business vs. workers" but "level playing field vs. cheap labor race to the bottom."

Political tactics

- Start local and municipal: cities and states often move faster and can provide proof points. A patchwork of local wins builds momentum and creates imitation effects.

- Build alliances with small-business groups and chambers interested in stable demand and reduced turnover.

- Put worker stories front-and-center to make the case human and relatable.

- Use employer champions who succeed after adapting: case studies weaken fear narratives.

2. Close tax loopholes and broaden the base

Why start here

Before you raise headline rates, close escape hatches. Loopholes produce perceived unfairness and fuel opposition: defenders say "we're just punishing investment," while the reality is tax systems let complex avoidance dilute revenue. Base-broadening is often the most politically defensible way to raise revenue, because it exposes unfair carve-outs and reduces the need for headline-grabbing rate increases.

Key targets to close (the usual suspects)

- **Carried interest and similar reclassifications** that let labor income be taxed as capital income.

- **Excessive depreciation benefits** for certain asset classes that create timing arbitrage.

- **Preferential treatment for certain investment vehicles** that are essentially consumption in disguise.

- **Like-kind exchange and step-up basis loopholes** that allow inter-generational tax avoidance.

- **Aggressive transfer pricing and use of offshore shells.** This is a cross-border problem requiring information exchange.

Design and enforcement steps

- **Adopt broad anti-abuse rules.** General anti-avoidance rules make purely form-over-substance arrangements harder.

- **Mandatory reporting and beneficial-ownership registries.** Transparency makes evasion more costly reputationally and legally.

- **Information-exchange treaties and coordination.** Work across borders to close digital-era arbitrage.

- **Tighten transfer-pricing rules.** Use safe-harbor thresholds and require contemporaneous documentation.

- **Sunset narrow carve-outs.** Each carve-out should require periodic renewal and public justification.

Sequencing

Close loopholes and strengthen the tax administration before raising large rates. That reduces leakage and undercuts narratives about capital flight. Start with the easiest-to-explain loopholes — those that look like obvious giveaways — to build public support.

Political tactics

- **Use examples.** Show how specific carve-outs benefit narrow interests (e.g., a special treatment that mainly helps a few hedge funds).

- **Link closing loopholes to visible uses.** "We'll use this revenue for childcare slots and tuition relief."

- **Partner with investigative journalists** who can expose avoidance stories to feed public pressure.

3. Implement higher marginal rates on top incomes (and align capital and labor taxation)

Why it works

Higher marginal rates on top incomes rebalance incentives at the margins: when very high incomes face modestly higher marginal rates, the revenue raised can fund public investment and curb inequality. Equally important is aligning tax treatment of capital income with labor income so that returns to ownership don't systematically receive discounts.

Design choices

- **Progressive top bands.** Add surtaxes above high thresholds (e.g., on incomes above $500k, $1m) as a politically feasible approach rather than a single steep top rate.

- **Capital income parity.** Tax long-term capital gains at rates closer to labor income rates, possibly with a slight preference to account for inflation and real long-term investment.

- **Minimum tax rules.** Impose a minimum effective tax on high-income taxpayers (e.g., a minimum percentage of total income).

- **Alternative Minimum Tax (AMT) refresh.** Ensure AMT or its equivalent catches planning that reduces effective rates substantially.

Implementation and enforcement

- **Declare the revenue uses up front.** People accept higher rates when they see tangible public benefits (education, health, infrastructure).

- **Close avoidance channels** simultaneously (see previous section).

- **Index thresholds to inflation** to avoid bracket creep politics and make policy predictable.

Political strategy

- Use surtaxes for specific purposes to build coalition — e.g., a "childcare and family support surtax" or "climate resilience surtax." Dedicated uses are easier to defend.

- Emphasize fairness and reciprocity: "We're asking a bit more from those who have benefited the most to build a more productive society."

- Pair with visible tax credits and benefits for middle-income households to reduce distributional anxiety.

4. Expand public services: healthcare, education, housing

Why these first

Public goods are the hardest-to-evade investments: they increase resilience, equalize opportunity, and provide visible returns. Investing in health, education, and housing both improves welfare and supports an economy where people can thrive and take risks.

Healthcare: Steps that scale politically

- **Lower out-of-pocket costs first.** Cap deductibles and co-pays for common services and medicines; negotiate bulk prices for drugs; expand generic availability.

- **Expand public coverage in targeted ways.** Extend public insurance to low- and middle-income groups in a phased approach (e.g., expand Medicaid-equivalent to near-poor). Where universal systems are politically feasible, build toward single-payer or public option models.

- **Use price transparency and negotiation.** Require price disclosure and empower public payers to negotiate rates with providers.

- **Invest in preventive care and primary care teams.** This reduces long-term costs and improves productivity.

Education: From pre-K through higher education

- **Early childhood care and education.** Invest in universal pre-K and subsidies for childcare — high social returns and hugely popular with parents.

- **K–12 equalization.** Reduce dependence on local property taxes by pooling baseline funding at higher levels and targeting additional resources to disadvantaged districts.

- **Make college affordable.** Expand public tuition support, reduce student loan burdens, and scale vocational and apprenticeship programs tied to local employment needs.

Housing: The basics of affordability

- **Preserve and expand affordable units.** Use public financing for construction and rehabilitation, support community land trusts, and fund inclusionary zoning programs.

- **Use rent subsidies with supply expansion.** Vouchers help households now while supply-side programs enlarge long-term stock.

- **Municipal power.** Unlock public land for affordable housing and prioritize long-term leases to community groups.

Financing and sequencing

- **Start with highly visible, low-friction items.** Expand child care slots; cap prescription drug costs for seniors; fund school support staff in struggling schools. Quick wins demonstrate competence.

- **Use a blended finance model.** Combine progressive revenue (see taxes above) with reallocation of inefficient subsidies, green bonds, and public bank financing.

- **Pilot and scale.** Start pilot programs in municipalities or regions to show proof-of-concept, maintain political flexibility, and reduce risk.

Political tactics

- **Build beneficiary coalitions.** Parents, elderly voters, teachers, and health care workers are natural allies.

- **Leverage employer interests.** Employers gain from healthier, more stable workforces. Recruit business leaders who benefit from reduced turnover to support public coverage and childcare expansions.

- **Frame investments as productivity and fairness.** Public spending is an investment in human capital that yields sustained returns.

5. Use public procurement to favor equitable practices

Why procurement matters

Public procurement—how government buys goods and services—is a huge lever. If public purchasing prioritizes firms that pay living wages, hire locally, use unions, or meet environmental standards, the public purse becomes a market-shaping tool that channels demand to equitable businesses.

Design elements

- **Living-wage and labor standards clauses.** Require contractors to meet wage floors and benefits standards.

- **Local and small-business preferences.** Use preference points or set-asides for small, local, or cooperative businesses.

- **Social impact criteria.** Include metrics like local hiring, apprenticeship programs, and supplier diversity in scoring.

- **Long-term contracts for local ecosystems.** Favor multi-year contracts with clause preventing race-to-bottom bidding.

Implementation and safeguards

- **Transparent bidding and metrics.** Publish procurement decisions and scoring rubrics so choices are contestable and visible.

- **Capacity-building grants.** Help small firms meet standards through technical assistance and financing, so rules don't become barriers.

- **Penalty and compliance regimes.** Enforce labor and environmental clauses with clear penalties.

Political tactics

- **Municipal pilots.** Cities can move faster and set examples (e.g., procurement rules for municipal services). Each municipal victory builds national momentum.

- **Employer coalition.** Engage responsible large firms that prefer stable, high-quality suppliers and want to avoid race-to-bottom pricing.

- **Use pilot success stories** to counter narratives that procurement reforms are inefficient.

---

6. Sequencing: the strategic order that makes the first swing effective

How you order reforms matters because each change shifts incentives and political landscapes. Here's a pragmatic sequencing that minimizes evasion opportunities and builds coalitions:

1. **Transparency & enforcement strengthening.** Beneficial-ownership registries, reporting requirements, and funding for tax administration and labor inspectors. (Without this, rate increases leak revenue; enforcement is the hinge of reform.)
2. **Local wage and procurement wins.** Launch municipal minimum-wage increases and procurement reforms. These are visible wins that build public support and practical models.
3. **Close glaring loopholes and broaden the tax base.** Do the obvious cleanups that are easy to explain and hard to defend (odd carve-outs, broken subsidies).
4. **Expand targeted public services.** Early childhood care, prescription caps, school support. Tangible benefits build middle-class support.
5. **Introduce moderate surtaxes or higher marginal rates with closed loopholes.** With enforcement in place and revenue uses popular, higher rates become politically achievable.
6. **Roll out wealth measures or minimum taxes on the ultra-wealthy, accompanied by international cooperation.** This step takes more time and

coordination, but it's politically plausible once the public sees benefits and transparency.

7. **Institutional reforms: antitrust, labor law modernization, national procurement standards.** These structural steps cement gains and reduce future capture.

The point is to lock leak-proof systems and visible public benefits before increasing the price for elites. That sequencing reduces escape options, builds credibility, and creates constituencies that will defend reforms.

7. Political tactics: coalition-building, messaging, and defensive planning

Build broad coalitions

- Unite workers, middle-income households, small-business owners, municipal leaders, faith groups, and community organizations.

- Pitch reforms in language that resonates across groups: security for families, stability for businesses, dignity for work, and sustainability for communities.

Messaging: frame and narratives

- **Frame as investment.** "We're investing in childcare, health, and schools so people can work and businesses can thrive."

- **Use reciprocity language.** "Those who benefited most help pay, and everyone benefits from safer streets, better schools, and stronger local economies."

- **Tell human stories.** Case studies of families helped by a higher minimum wage or a new childcare slot make impacts emotionally real.

- **Be pre-emptive on fears.** Prepare data and examples showing minimal job losses, benefits to small businesses, and actual employer adaptations.

Defensive planning

- **Legal-defense funds.** Expect litigation and prepare legal teams from the start.

- **Rapid-response media.** Counter PR attacks quickly with evidence and stories.

- **Transparency as armor.** Publish revenue and spending plans; keep procurement open and auditable.

- **International coordination.** For wealth and tax measures, work with international partners to reduce flight options.

8. Measuring success and building accountability

Good policy needs good metrics. Early monitoring shows success, builds public support, and provides ammunition against rollback.

Core indicators

- **Poverty and low-income rates** (absolute and relative).
- **Median wages and wage growth** (especially for bottom and middle deciles).
- **Employment rates and hours worked.**
- **Tax revenue collected from targeted measures** and measures of tax gap.
- **Service access metrics**: childcare slots per 1,000 children, uninsured rates, affordable housing units created.
- **Procurement outcomes**: share of contracts to local/co-op/small firms, job quality metrics among contractors.
- **Enforcement outcomes**: numbers of inspections, violations found, recoveries, and penalties.

Use dashboards and publish regular progress reports. Transparent metrics make it harder for opponents to spin failure narratives and allow advocates to adjust policy design quickly.

9. A composite first-swing timeline (illustrative, not prescriptive)

This is a compact way to imagine sequencing — a hypothetical 2-year start that builds credibility:

- **Months 1–3:** Executive orders for transparency (beneficial ownership; procurement transparency); budget request to expand tax administration and labor inspection; launch media campaign on shared-investment framing.

- **Months 4–9:** Municipal minimum-wage legislation in several cities; procurement pilot for living-wage contracts; start childcare expansion pilots; announce closure of glaring loopholes (fast, easy wins).

- **Months 10–18:** Introduce surtaxes on top incomes with detailed revenue use plans (childcare and housing); concurrently pass enforcement budget bills and anti-abuse tax provisions; publicize early wins and employer success stories.

- **Months 18–24:** Expand coverage of public services (scale childcare and housing programs); start international talks on information exchange and minimum taxation for coordinated wealth measures; begin drafting longer-term antitrust and labor modernization bills backed by demonstrated popular support.

Adapt the timeline to institutional realities; cycles, elections, and legal constraints will vary. The point: early wins plus enforcement credibility unlock deeper changes.

10. The first swing is more than a policy set — it's a political technology

A first swing that breaks a chunk of the piñata is both policy and politics. It must improve lives now, make evasion harder, build stable constituencies, and set up infrastructure for later, deeper change. The measures in this chapter are practical and complementary: wages that lift demand, taxes and enforcement that fund public goods, services that reduce inequality and expand opportunity, procurement that rewards fairness, and sequencing that prevents capture.

Remember: you're not aiming for pure purity. Politics requires compromise, but the aim is to avoid compromises that hollow reform. Design for enforceability, transparency, accountability, and coalition durability. Measure relentlessly. Tell stories that people can feel and believe. Anticipate the counterattack and prepare legal and narrative defenses.

This first swing needn't break the whole piñata. It must do two things: put candy in people's hands, and change expectations. When households see their wages rise, their child gets care, and their local school gets repairs — and when wealthy actors cannot hide what they own — the political landscape changes. The next swings become easier. The piñata becomes less defensible, not because we outspend the empire of influence, but because a democratic majority sees a better alternative and will fight to keep it.

Grab the stick with clarity, and swing with strategy.

Technology, Platforms, and the Piñata

Technology is not neutral. The same code, servers, and protocols can either cement a fortified piñata or pry it open. Over the last two decades, digital platforms—search, social media, marketplaces, app stores, cloud providers, and financial protocols—have remade economic and political life. They created enormous consumer convenience and new opportunities for entrepreneurship, but they also created new vectors for concentration: gatekeeping monopolies, data hoarding, algorithmic rent extraction, surveillance-enabled power, and transnational regulatory arbitrage. At the same time, the same technologies enable alternatives: platform cooperatives, open-source commons, decentralized finance experiments, and powerful new organizing tools for movements. This chapter maps that duality—how tech fortifies and how it can dismantle—and then offers concrete policy and design proposals to democratize digital infrastructure so it favors shared prosperity rather than concentrated capture.

We'll move through four parts: (1) how platforms fortify the piñata (market power, data concentration, algorithmic control, surveillance, and regulatory arbitrage); (2) how technology can be reparative (platform co-ops, open source, public digital infrastructure, DeFi with guardrails, digital organizing); (3) concrete policy and design proposals to democratize tech (competition rules, data governance, public digital goods, worker ownership, standards for interoperability and portability, civic procurement, and platform labor rules); and (4) practical sequencing and political tactics for making change stick.

Part I — How Platforms Fortify the Piñata

1. Gatekeepers, network effects, and the gravity of winner-take-most markets

Digital platforms tend to produce winner-take-most outcomes. Network effects—where a platform's value to each user grows as more users join—create feedback loops that make it easy for a leading firm to entrench itself. Once a platform becomes the default for search, app distribution, social graphs, or e-commerce, it gains advantages that are hard to dislodge: user attention, third-party integrations, developer ecosystems, and control over complementary markets (ads, payments, cloud services). The European Digital Markets Act (DMA) explicitly recognizes this dynamic and designates "gatekeepers" whose core platform services impose de facto market power; the law requires those gatekeepers to follow interoperability, non-self-preferencing, and portability rules to preserve contestability. The EU's designation of several large firms as gatekeepers—the big handful that dominate search, app ecosystems, social networks, and marketplaces—illustrates the structural reality regulators now confront.

In the United States and elsewhere, regulators and courts have begun to assert that dominant platforms exercise monopoly power—not only in price terms but in the ability to shape markets and lock in users. Ongoing antitrust litigation and investigations against major tech firms reflect sustained concern about gatekeeping, exclusivity deals, and the sprawling bundling of services that raise entry barriers for rivals. Even when courts stop short of breakups, the fact of sustained legal pressure signals that market structure matters for democracy and fair economic outcomes.

Why does this fortify the piñata? Defaults capture choice. If you must go through a gatekeeper for distribution, discovery, or payments, you are subject to its rules—pricing, algorithms, data demands, and contractual terms. Over time those rules concentrate rents upward: app revenues flow to owners; advertising yields go to platforms; and small suppliers and workers find their bargaining power reduced.

2. Data hoarding: from attention to ownership

Data is platform fuel. The more a platform knows about what you search, buy, click, and watch, the better it can match ads, recommend content, and optimize supply. That information advantage creates a two-fold problem. First, it amplifies market power: insights about user behavior enable superior ad targeting and product design that competitors cannot easily replicate. Second, it converts user data—and the labor of producing it—into rents captured by platform owners. The economic value of personalized advertising and algorithmic recommendation flows to those who own the data infrastructure; producers, workers, and users rarely capture commensurate returns for the data they generate.

Data concentration is not an abstract concern. Policy experiments (like data portability, interoperability mandates, and public data trusts) aim to break that concentration by making data more fluid and accessible for public-interest uses and competitive entry. The DMA's obligations, for instance, explicitly include data-use transparency and certain portability requirements to reduce lock-in. Those moves are an explicit recognition that data hoarding functions as a long-lasting fortification around the piñata.

3. Algorithmic gatekeeping and opacity

Algorithms decide more and more of what people see and buy. They rank search results, curate feeds, set ad auctions, recommend products, and even inform hiring and lending decisions. Yet the logic of these algorithms is often proprietary and opaque. Opacity has two effects: it lowers accountability when algorithms produce discriminatory or extractive outcomes, and it increases the capacity of platforms to tilt markets through self-preferencing rules and promoted-placement mechanics that favor the platform's own services or well-resourced advertisers.

Opaque algorithmic governance thus becomes its own fortification: even when regulators or competitors could challenge a platform on merits, the black-box nature of ranking, recommendation, and auction systems insulates powerful actors. Calls for algorithmic transparency, auditability, and explainability are attempts to make this layer of the fortification permeable.

4. Surveillance and behavioral control as private infrastructure

Platform revenues depend on attention and engagement. To sustain and monetize attention, firms build sophisticated surveillance architectures that track behavior across devices and contexts, infer tastes and vulnerabilities, and feed that intelligence back into persuasive design. That infrastructure is often embedded into the broader internet ecosystem—through cookies, SDKs, third-party trackers, and ad-tech chains—magnifying the surveillance reach beyond the owning firm.

Surveillance architectures do real social work: they guide attention, nudge behavior, influence political opinion, and shape market demand. When a few firms own the lenses through which most people experience the web, the political economy of attention becomes a source of concentrated power. Regulations that limit pervasive tracking, require consented use, or create privacy-by-default models reduce the ability of private platforms to direct social attention as they wish.

5. Platform labor and governance: weakening worker voice

Platforms reshape labor markets. On the one hand, they create flexible income opportunities; on the other, they drive down bargaining power through algorithmic management, subcontracting, and classification as independent contractors. The gig economy's business model often externalizes costs (benefits, training, scheduling risk) while centralizing matching and price-setting power into the platform. This "two-sided" model lets platforms extract rents from both demand and supply sides while avoiding the legal responsibilities and fixed costs associated with employment.

Platform governance choices—opaque ratings, unilateral deactivations, dynamic pricing algorithms—give platforms outsized power over worker livelihoods, limiting effective collective action. Worker voice is further weakened when platform terms are non-negotiable and communication channels are unidirectional. Strengthening worker rights, transparency in algorithmic management, and collective forms of ownership or co-determination can blunt these effects and restore bargaining power.

6. Regulatory arbitrage and transnational shielding

Platforms operate globally. When national rules bite, firms can shift activity, data storage, or corporate entities to more permissive jurisdictions. Tax avoidance, data-routing, and legal forum shopping are classic arbitrage strategies that protect fortified advantage. The transnational nature of digital platforms thus amplifies the piñata's fortifications: if one country tightens rules, platforms can often adapt in ways that preserve core rents unless international coordination reduces arbitrage opportunities. Hence the push for cross-border instruments—data-sharing agreements, minimum tax regimes, and cooperative enforcement—aimed at reducing the ability of platforms to exploit jurisdictional seams.

Part II — How Technology Can Break the Piñata

The same technologies that fortify can also democratize. Below are the constructive architectures and movements that make digital infrastructure friendlier to shared prosperity.

1. Platform cooperatives and democratic ownership

Platform cooperativism reimagines the platform model with democratic governance and shared ownership—workers, users, and communities own the platform and share in the surplus. Platform co-ops exist as ride-hail alternatives, local marketplaces, and service platforms that prioritize equitable pay, transparent rules, and local reinvestment. The Platform Cooperativism Consortium and OECD analyses document growing interest, practical toolkits, and pilot examples that show this model's feasibility. Platform co-ops are not a panacea—they face scaling challenges and capital constraints—but they offer a meaningful counter-model where the benefits of networked markets diffuse to those who contribute.

Examples range from driver-owned taxi apps to cooperative housing rental platforms and care co-ops. Public policy can accelerate platform co-ops with start-up financing, procurement preferences, technical assistance, and legal forms that make democratic governance easier to scale.

2. Open-source software and public digital commons

The open-source movement has already delivered critical public goods—Linux, Apache, PostgreSQL, and countless libraries—that underpin much of modern infrastructure. Open-source principles—transparency, collaborative governance, and shared stewardship—produce software that can be audited, forked, and improved by communities rather than controlled by single firms. Publicly funded open-source projects and standards bodies create a durable commons that reduces vendor lock-in and gives public agencies and small firms alternatives to proprietary platforms.

Public investment in open-source infrastructure (from identity layers to secure messaging and mapping) democratizes foundational technology and reduces the power asymmetries that come from private control. Open standards and reference implementations make interoperability easier and lower the cost of entry for smaller players.

3. Decentralized finance (DeFi) and the promise—and perils—of decentralization

DeFi proposes financial services without traditional intermediaries, using smart contracts and blockchains. In principle, DeFi can democratize access to credit, payments, and investment by removing gatekeeper intermediaries and making financial rails programmable and composable. However, the experience to date shows both promise and serious risks: liquidity fragility, governance centralization through token distributions, exploitable smart-contract bugs, abuse by illicit actors, and the "decentralization illusion" where protocols still depend on centralized teams and off-chain actors. Major international institutions (IMF, BIS, national treasuries) call for regulatory frameworks that reduce money-laundering risks, improve consumer protections, and ensure financial stability while not unduly stifling innovation. Thoughtful DeFi policy can harness the technology's empowering potential while mitigating runaway systemic risks.

4. Public-interest platforms and municipal digital infrastructure

Cities and public utilities can build digital platforms for transit, housing allocation, licensing, and community services that prioritize accessibility and democratic governance rather than extraction. Municipal broadband projects, public identity services, and city procurement platforms keep value local and create alternatives to private gatekeepers. These public-interest platforms carry potential multiplier effects—lower costs, increased civic participation, and better integration of social services.

5. Digital organizing, decentralized coordination, and movement power

Digital tools amplify organizing capacity. Social media, encrypted messaging, peer-to-peer fundraising platforms, and mapping tools let movements coordinate quickly, narrate stories to large audiences, and scale local wins into national waves. The past decade's labor and social movements show the power of digital organizing to mobilize, recruit, and coordinate pressure—while also reminding us that online activity must be tethered to offline organizing to create durable institutional change. Evidence shows that digital mobilization improves outreach and rapid coordination but must be combined with on-the-ground relationship building and legal capacity for lasting wins.

Part III — Policy & Design Proposals to Democratize Tech

If technology's architecture shapes outcomes, then policy and design can shift incentives and structures. Below are concrete proposals—actionable, combinable, and tailored to blunt fortifications and amplify democratic uses.

1. Modernize competition law for platformed markets

Policy goals. Update antitrust and competition policy to account for multi-sided platforms, data advantages, and serial acquisitions of nascent rivals.

Specific proposals.

- Adopt merger-review standards that include effects on data concentration, network effects, and nascent-competitor elimination—sometimes called "killer acquisitions." Use broader metrics (entry barriers, developer ecosystems, downstream impacts) rather than narrow short-term price tests.
- Create presumptions against certain bundling and self-preferencing practices by dominant gatekeepers—demand interop and neutral ranking as default.
- Empower ex post and ex ante tools: stronger merger review, the ability to impose interoperability obligations, and behavioral remedies where structural remedies are impractical.

Design notes. Antitrust changes require institutional capacity—staff with data-science expertise and global coordination to handle cross-border firms. The European DMA model—designation of gatekeepers and obligations to preserve contestability—offers one template for blending ex ante obligations with enforcement.

2. Data governance for empowerment, not enclosure

Policy goals. Shift data from hoarded asset to governed resource: enable portability, consented use, and public-interest re-use.

Specific proposals.

- Enact strong data portability and interoperability mandates for gatekeepers to allow users to move profiles, social graphs, and content between platforms in usable formats.
- Require data-use transparency: clear, machine-readable disclosures of how data is used for ad targeting, ranking, and pricing.
- Create public-interest data trusts: neutral custodians that manage anonymized datasets for research, anti-monopoly enforcement, and public-service innovation under strict governance and privacy safeguards.

- Expand rights to repair and reverse-engineer algorithmic outputs where necessary for accountability (with safeguards for IP and safety).

Design notes. Portability reduces lock-in, interoperability lowers switching costs, and public-data trusts help under-resourced researchers and regulators understand platform market dynamics. The DMA and GDPR show legal levers already exist but need broader enforcement and implementation to be effective.

3. Public digital infrastructure and open-source investment

Policy goals. Build digital public goods so that essential services aren't mediated only by private platforms.

Specific proposals.

- Fund open-source infrastructure (identity systems, secure messaging backbones, urban mobility APIs) through public grants and institutional support.

- Create public code and standards repositories (with professional maintenance funding) so governments and small businesses can rely on robust, vetted implementations instead of proprietary stacks.

- Use conditional public procurement funds to require open standards and non-proprietary APIs, reducing vendor lock-in and creating interoperable ecosystems.

Design notes. Public funding must follow governance: long-term maintenance budgets, transparent roadmaps, and community stewardship are key to avoiding the "orphaned open source" problem where projects outlive funding and rot.

4. Platform labor rights and governance redesign

Policy goals. Strengthen bargaining power and transparency for platform-dependent workers; enable collective decision-making and worker-ownership paths.

Specific proposals.

- Legally enforce algorithmic transparency for platforms' workforce-management systems—what metrics drive deactivation, surge pricing, or task allocation—and mandate human appeal processes.

- Provide a legal path for collective bargaining for gig workers, and consider sectoral bargaining models for platform-dominated sectors.

- Offer tax incentives and procurement preferences for worker-owned or cooperative platforms; create public funds to finance worker buyouts of distressed platform-dependent businesses.

- Require portability of reputation data: worker ratings should be transferable between platforms to reduce dependence and ease mobility.

Design notes. These measures combine labor law updates with procurement strategy and finance support to make worker ownership feasible.

5. Regulated, accountable DeFi and public-finance interfaces

Policy goals. Capture the efficiency and inclusion potential of programmable finance while ensuring consumer protection, AML/KYC compliance, and systemic safeguards.

Specific proposals.

- Create regulatory sandboxes that let DeFi protocols operate under supervised conditions while they build audited security, governance, and reserves.

- Require transparent governance mechanisms for token-based DAOs, including quorum rules, disclosure of major holders, and backstop arrangements where protocols manage liabilities.

- Integrate DeFi with public-CBDC pilots where central banks provide settlement rails for stable and accountable execution.

Design notes. DeFi policy must balance innovation and mitigation. Global coordination on AML/CTF and custody rules prevents arbitrage and illicit use.

6. Interoperability, APIs, and mandated non-discrimination

Policy goals. Reduce gatekeeper power by requiring technical interoperability and non-discriminatory treatment of third parties.

Specific proposals.

- Mandate standard APIs to let third-party services interoperate with essential platform functions (messaging, discovery, payments) under fair, reasonable, and non-discriminatory terms.

- Ban self-preferencing where the platform's own services are ranked ahead of rivals without legitimate relevance or user choice.

- Back API mandates with enforcement and technical standards development communities to ensure safe, secure implementations.

Design notes. Interoperability must be implemented securely to prevent abuse; minimum standards and auditability are crucial.

7. Civic procurement and public-platform default

Policy goals. Use public buying power to create space for non-extractive, locally accountable platforms.

Specific proposals.

- Require public agencies to prefer open-source and cooperative platforms for public-service delivery unless a clear efficiency case exists.

- Bundle procurement across municipalities to create scale for public-interest platforms and co-ops.

Design notes. Procurement policy is a lever that creates real demand for alternative models and helps them scale.

Part IV — Sequencing, Tactics, and Political Strategy

Design matters, but so does sequencing. You do not dismantle a fortified machine by attacking the outermost layer first. Here's a pragmatic path:

1. **Build public digital goods and pilots.** Start with municipal broadband, public procurement of open-source tools, and funding for platform co-op pilots. Quick wins create examples and constituencies.
2. **Transparency and enforcement upgrades.** Implement beneficial-ownership equivalent for algorithms: require disclosure of ranking criteria and ad-auction rules in machine-readable form for regulators. Strengthen data- and consumer-protection enforcement.
3. **Interoperability and portability mandates.** With

robust public alternatives and oversight capacity in place, require gatekeepers to open key interfaces under fair terms.

4. **Labor and governance rights.** Introduce portability of reputation, worker governance pilots, and sectoral bargaining frameworks; pair with procurement preference for co-ops.
5. **Competition law reform and cross-border coordination.** Update merger-review standards and coordinate internationally on data, taxation, and enforcement to reduce arbitrage.
6. **Scale responsible decentralization.** Regulate DeFi with sandboxes, backstops, and public-finance interfaces while supporting transparent, audited protocols.

Political tactics to accompany this sequence include narrative framing (tech as infrastructure and public-commons, not only profit), coalition-building (workers, developers, small businesses, privacy advocates, municipal leaders), and using municipalities as laboratories to demonstrate models. Tactical litigation and strategic rulemaking can bind firms to obligations while creating standards for wider adoption.

Part V — A Practical Example: Turning a Municipal Market

Imagine a city that wants to reduce reliance on a dominant ride-hail firm, improve workers' pay, and capture more local value. A multi-pronged approach could look like this:

- City funds a platform co-op incubator, offering low-interest loans and technical support to driver-led cooperatives.

- Public procurement guarantees ride volume (airport and city-contracted shuttle services) to the co-op on a multi-year contract if service metrics are met.

- The city passes an ordinance requiring driver-rating portability between platforms and algorithmic transparency for dispatch systems serving municipal services.

- The city uses its purchasing power to insist that third-party apps interoperate with the co-op's dispatch API, increasing rider choice.

- Simultaneously the state updates labor law to allow sectoral bargaining for transport services, creating a floor across apps and co-ops.

This bundle reduces switching costs, creates demand, strengthens worker bargaining, and demonstrates that alternatives can be viable at scale. It also makes regulatory capture or litigation more politically costly for incumbents.

Technology as Political Economy

Technology is not destiny. The architectures we build—code, standards, markets, and institutions—embed political and economic choices. Platforms can be designed to centralize rents or distribute value; they can be shaped to surveil or to empower. The policies above are not merely regulatory checklists; they are design principles for a democratic digital economy: portability and interoperability to reduce lock-in; public investment in open-source to create alternatives; labor rights and governance reforms to rebalance power; competition policy updated for networked markets; and careful regulation of novel financial rails to protect people while enabling innovation.

If the piñata is to be opened more widely, we must treat digital infrastructure as a collective good worth defending. That means public investment, legal muscle, and political imagination. It also means building alternatives that show, empirically and locally, that a different technological future is not only possible but better for most people. Get the design right, deploy the policy tools in sequence, and use public procurement, labor law, and open standards to scale democratic models. The stick of the future is not a single weapon; it's a set of interoperable instruments—legal, technical, political—that, wielded together, can pry open a hardened piñata and let the candy circulate again.

Global Piñata Economics — Climate & International Solidarity

The world's piñata is global. Candy flows across borders: investment, profits, tax rules, corporate power, debt contracts, and greenhouse gases. That means the fix can't be purely local. You can raise wages in one country, claw back some taxes in another, or build municipal public goods — and those things matter. But if the mechanisms that hoard candy (offshore secrecy, cross-border profit-shifting, unfair trade and debt architectures, and climate inequality) operate at transnational scale, then so must the remedies. This chapter places redistribution in a global context: it explains how tax havens, capital flight, trade rules, and debt traps fortify the piñata; it shows why climate justice requires transfers rather than loans; and it makes the case for coordinated international measures — practical, politically realistic, and institutionally specific — to stop flight and enable a credible program of global redistribution.

We begin with the blunt fact that much of the world's wealth is hidden, untaxed, or sheltered from ordinary democratic control. That matters because the effective global fiscal base is smaller than it ought to be, leaving poorer countries strapped for revenue while private fortunes roam free. We then walk through the levers that can change the balance: transparency and automatic information exchange, a global minimum tax, a strengthened international debt architecture, a scaled-up system of climate transfers (grants, loss & damage financing), and coordinated trade and development policies that prioritize capacity-building and fair rules. Along the way we treat political feasibility seriously — showing what's already moving and how to build alliances to push the rest forward.

1. The Global Scale of Hoarding: What's Hidden, and Why It Matters

Start with a simple arithmetic shock: tens of trillions of dollars of private financial wealth have been held offshore or in jurisdictions where it escapes ordinary tax scrutiny. If you accept even conservative estimates, the sum is large enough to reshape global public finance if it were taxed or transparently reported. Researchers such as Gabriel Zucman and teams at tax observatories have documented the scale of offshore wealth and the concentration of that wealth at the very top of the distribution. This is not abstract: it means lower revenue for public schools, health systems, and infrastructure in poor countries, even while global richest households accumulate more influence and capital.

The mechanisms are straightforward. Multinational firms shift profits through intra-company pricing and tax planning; wealthy individuals hold assets in complex trusts, shell companies, and secrecy jurisdictions that deny tax authorities visibility; and digital and financial innovations open new routes to hide or re-characterize income. Those practices are legal in many places thanks to rules and loopholes, and illegal evasion is sometimes trivial to hide behind layers of corporate ownership. Whatever you call it — sheltering, avoidance, or evasion — the practical result is the same: private claims on global value that are not subject to democratic taxation and redistribution.

Two consequences follow. First, the fiscal space for public investment in low- and middle-income countries is constrained. Those countries have to spend precious revenue covering debt service, import bills, and interest payments instead of schools and health. Second, the political economy shifts: wealth that can move across borders buys influence in multiple jurisdictions and escapes domestic accountability. If local leaders cannot tax powerful actors, public legitimacy frays.

2. Tax Havens, Global Minimum Tax, and the Limits of National-Only Strategies

You can legislate domestically all you like, but multinational tax planning and secrecy jurisdictions will blunt the effects. That's why the international architecture of taxation matters.

The global minimum tax: a necessary first step

The OECD/G20 "two-pillar" agreement — and specifically the global minimum tax (Pillar Two) — is an important institutional innovation because it recognizes the problem of competitive tax races and profit shifting. A coordinated minimum tax rate applied to large multinationals reduces the incentive to route income through low-tax jurisdictions and narrows the room for arbitrage. Implementation has been uneven and complex, but it is an operational example of countries choosing collective action over unilateral tax competition.

A credible minimum tax does three things: it raises effective tax floors, it makes domestic rate increases more feasible (because the risk of capital flight declines), and it reduces the fiscal drag that offshore profit shifting imposes on many countries. But it is not a silver bullet. Pillar Two currently targets large multinationals and has many carve-outs; it does not capture private individual wealth, nor does it eliminate secrecy in small-jurisdiction structures.

Beyond the minimum: transparency, beneficial ownership, and automatic exchange

To get at hidden wealth you need transparency in ownership and automatic exchange of information. Public beneficial-ownership registries, automatic reporting from financial institutions (the Common Reporting Standard or CRS), and country-by-country reporting for corporations empower tax authorities to follow the money. The academic and policy literature shows that disclosure reduces evasion and increases political pressure to tax appropriately. The goal is to convert hidden, opaque holdings into visible claims that national authorities — and international partners — can assess.

Withholding and source rules

Another pragmatic tool is withholding taxes applied at source for certain cross-border payments (interest, royalties, dividends) where beneficial ownership is unclear. Withholding creates a friction that discourages tax arbitrage unless proper disclosure is made. Coupled with transparency and enforcement, withholdings can be designed as temporary brakes while more permanent reporting systems are scaled up.

The role of wealthy "haven" jurisdictions

Secrecy jurisdictions maintain the global fortification because they profit from providing opacity and legal shelters. Tackling them requires a mixture of carrots (incentives to reform), sticks (sanctions, blacklists, and countermeasures), and multilateral bargaining that makes non-compliance costly. This is politically fraught — some advanced economies have been slow to crack down when their own financial centers profit — but recent momentum in the OECD framework and tax cooperation suggests the politics can shift if civil society pressure and credible enforcement align.

3. Debt, Debt Service, and the Common Framework: Why Global Debt Architecture Matters

Capital flight and tax avoidance compound the debt problem. Low- and middle-income countries face debt-service burdens that crowd out public investment, and the global debt architecture for restructuring has proven slow and politically awkward.

The failure of narrow, creditor-led processes

The Debt Service Suspension Initiative and the G20's Common Framework were designed to prevent sovereign defaults during COVID and to create a process for restructuring. In practice, however, restructurings have been slow and incomplete, with many cases delayed by complex negotiations among official and private creditors. The Zambia restructuring case illustrates progress and the pain of drawn-out process: it was a milestone but also exposed the Common Framework's limits — particularly the late involvement of private creditors and the lack of a standing, fast mechanism for coordination. Observers from the World Bank and IMF have criticized the sluggishness and argued for quicker, more comprehensive approaches.

A better global debt workout mechanism

The global piñata will stay fortified while debt servicing siphons resources to creditors rather than public goods. Reform options include: (a) a standing international debt-restructuring mechanism with clear rules and impartial arbitration that binds private creditors; (b) mandatory participation clauses for private creditors when official multilateral aid or financing is being restructured; (c) expedited timelines; and (d) mechanisms to ensure restructurings are oriented to debt sustainability while preserving social investment and climate adaptation needs.

A stronger mechanism needs political buy-in from creditor countries (including China, the U.S., and EU members) and institutional backing (IMF, World Bank, a UN-facilitated process). It should also include stronger contingent financing tied to investment in public goods, not just fiscal consolidation.

SDR reallocations and replenishing fiscal space

The IMF's 2021 SDR allocation showed how supranational liquidity creation can boost global reserves. Proposals to reallocate SDRs from wealthy countries to poorer ones, or to channel SDRs into climate and development funds, have been politically controversial but technically possible. Advocates argue that reallocated SDRs can provide low-cost liquidity that avoids adding to debtor burdens. More ambitious proposals include new SDR issuances or an IMF facility dedicated to climate-resilient financing. Those are politically feasible only if influential shareholders (notably the U.S.) consent; building the coalition for that consent is a central political task.

4. Trade Rules, Development, and Fair Bargains

Trade rules are not neutral. Tariff schedules, rules of origin, intellectual property (IP) regimes, and regulatory harmonization shape what developing countries can produce and export. Historically, wealthy economies wrote the rules in ways that favored their industrial structures. Today the problem is subtler but still real: complex compliance requirements, investor-state dispute clauses, and aggressive IP protections can restrict policy space for industrial policy, local value capture, and public-interest regulation.

Rethinking trade for development

A global redistribution strategy should include revising trade rules to allow developing countries fiscal and policy space to build domestic industries. Practical proposals include:

- **Reforming rules of origin** so that regional value chains are not penalized.

- **Limiting the reach of investor-state dispute settlement (ISDS)** provisions that can chill public-interest regulation.

- **Easing IP barriers for public goods** (e.g., vaccines and climate technologies) when those are necessary for public welfare and adaptation — the COVID-era TRIPS waiver debate is an example of where global solidarity matters in practice.

- **Preferential procurement and rules favoring regional integration** that allow countries to build domestic capabilities.

Trade rules can be rebalanced to treat development as a primary objective, not an afterthought.

5. Climate Justice: Finance, Loss & Damage, and the Case for Transfers

Climate change is the quintessential global redistribution problem. The countries that contributed least to historical greenhouse gas emissions suffer earliest and most. Adaptation, mitigation, and loss & damage demand large-scale transfers — not loans that worsen debt burdens.

Public finance, not private debt

The Green Climate Fund (GCF) and similar multilateral mechanisms are important but underfunded relative to the scale of need. The GCF's replenishments have raised billions (GCF-2 pledges in the low tens of billions), but those amounts fall short of the trillions needed annually for adaptation and equitable mitigation pathways. Grants matter more than loans for the most vulnerable because loans add to debt distress.

Loss & damage and contractual justice

The political breakthrough of a formal loss & damage mechanism that channels finance to countries suffering irreversible climate harms is critical. That finance must be predictable, adequate, and not conditioned on austerity. It should include direct grants, insured risk-transfer mechanisms, and dedicated rebuild funds. The moral case for transfers aligns with self-interest: a destabilized region has spillovers — migration, political instability, and supply-chain shocks — that affect wealthy and poor countries alike.

Green conditionality that is fair

When climate finance does come from multilateral lenders, conditionality should promote social investment and climate-resilient development, not cutbacks. Financing should be accompanied by technical transfer, debt relief tied to climate vulnerability, and investment in public infrastructure (grid resilience, water systems) that reduces long-term costs and increases social returns.

6. A Practical Package: Coordinated International Measures

Let me be concrete. A credible global redistribution program needs several coordinated elements that reinforce one another. Below is a practical package — a mix of institutional reforms, fiscal measures, and enforcement steps — that, taken together, reduce capital flight and create fiscal space for redistribution.

A. Global transparency and ownership registers

- **Universal beneficial-ownership registries**: public or access-regulated registries revealing ultimate owners of companies, trusts, and real estate entities. Jurisdictions that do not comply face graduated countermeasures (withholding taxes, denial of treaty benefits, reputational sanctions).

- **Automatic exchange of beneficial-ownership info and financial-account information** through standardized protocols (expanding CRS and FATCA-like sharing multilaterally).

- **Country-by-country reporting publicly available** for multinationals to allow scrutiny of where profit, payroll, and substantive economic activity are reported.

Rationale. Visibility reduces hiding, aids enforcement, empowers civil-society oversight, and makes tax avoidance politically costly. It is a precondition for credible global tax enforcement.

B. A strengthened global minimum tax with anti-abuse features

- **Make Pillar Two robust**, reduce carve-outs, and include mechanisms for taxing income of private wealth vehicles where appropriate.

- **Introduce an international enforcement compact** that denies treaty benefits to jurisdictions that facilitate treaty-shopping and profit-shifting.

- **Create a dispute-resolution mechanism** for cross-border tax rulings and a channel for developing countries to seek technical assistance.

Rationale. A durable floor reduces the option value of secrecy jurisdictions and helps stabilize global tax revenues.

C. An international debt-restructuring mechanism

- **Create a standing, impartial Debt Adjustment Court or tribunal** under UN or IMF auspices with clear timelines for creditor participation and legally binding decisions.

- **Mandate inclusion of private bondholders early in restructuring talks**, with standardized haircut and exchange frameworks to reduce delays.

- **Link debt relief to climate and development investments**, so restructurings free space for social and green spending.

Rationale. Predictable, fast debt workouts reduce the social cost of crises, limit opportunism, and free funds for public investment.

D. SDR reallocation and new international liquidity tools

- **Encourage wealthy-country rechanneling** of SDR allocations to a climate and development fund (via concessional loans, grants, or transfers) while preserving liquidity for recipient countries.

- **Consider a dedicated SDR issuance for climate adaptation**, with a governance framework prioritizing the most vulnerable.

Rationale. New liquidity can shore up reserves, finance adaptation, and avoid debt traps.

E. Climate finance as grant-based, scaled, and predictable

- **Scale up Green Climate Fund and multilateral climate finance**, prioritize grants over loans for vulnerable low-income countries.

- **Create a global loss & damage facility** with predictable replenishment and direct access for affected countries.

- **Integrate climate finance with debt relief** to avoid creating new debt burdens.

Rationale. Climate shocks are not the recipient's fault; grants and transfers are ethically defensible and economically efficient.

F. Trade rules for development

- **Enable policy space** for industrial policy and local content requirements where these promote social development.

- **Waive certain IP protections for public-interest technologies** (vaccines, key climate technologies) on a temporary, needs-based basis.

- **Support regional value-chain development** with technical assistance and preferential procurement.

Rationale. Development requires policy space and technology transfer; trade rules should not lock in dependency.

G. Coordinated enforcement and sanctions for secrecy jurisdictions

- **Design graded countermeasures** for noncompliant jurisdictions (tax withholding, financial penalties, restricted access to treaties).

- **Support asset-recovery mechanisms** and criminal-finance cooperation treaties to repatriate illicitly taken wealth — with a share returned to origin countries for public investment.

Rationale. Effective countermeasures change the incentive structure that keeps secrecy jurisdictions economically viable.

7. Politics: Building the Coalitions for Global Action

You'll notice that the package above is ambitious and requires coalition-building across rich and poor countries — and inside states among civil society, progressive business interests, and policy elites. That's difficult but not impossible. Modern momentum shows this: the OECD's minimum tax, the IMF SDR allocation, and GCF replenishments are proof that multilateral agreements can advance when political actors see common interest or are pressured by domestic constituencies.

Domestic politics matter

Wealth at home will resist global measures. Building domestic coalitions is essential: link redistribution to visible benefits (public health, climate resilience, education) and show taxpayers how global cooperation prevents tax flight and levels the playing field for honest domestic firms. Narratives that frame international action as reciprocal and fairness-based — "we protect our citizens from unfair competition; we help the vulnerable abroad" — can build wider support.

South–South coalitions

Low- and middle-income countries can coordinate to demand better deals. Regional groupings (African Union, ASEAN, Mercosur) can combine bargaining power to push for technology transfers, concessional financing, and fair trade terms.

Private-sector allies

Some business groups benefit from transparency and level playing fields — small and medium enterprises that lose to tax-avoiding multinationals, or local manufacturers disadvantaged by unfair competition. Engage these constituencies as part of broader coalitions.

Civil society and transnational advocacy

Global movements — unions, faith groups, environmental NGOs — can create public pressure and hold governments accountable. Campaigns that expose hidden wealth and show human consequences of austerity build moral force.

8. Implementation hurdles and how to manage them

Ambition bumps into reality: political resistance, enforcement constraints, and the risk of unintended consequences loom. Practical design must anticipate these problems.

- **Avoid one-size-fits-all.** Rules must be adapted to capacity: technical assistance and financing should help low-capacity countries implement reporting and enforcement.

- **Phase implementation.** Start with transparency and data-exchange (which, once institutionalized, makes enforcement easier), then layer on tax and withholding rules.

- **Protect policy space.** Trade and investment rules must explicitly preserve the right to pursue development-oriented regulation and environmental protection.

- **Guard against regulatory capture.** International institutions need independent monitoring, whistleblower protections, and civil-society access.
- **Measure outcomes.** Track revenue recovered, climate funds disbursed, poverty impacts, and debt-service savings; publish results to sustain political support.

9. What Redistribution Looks Like in Practice

The end-goal is not symbolic accounting but concrete redistribution that changes lives. Imagine a plausible scenario ten years into a serious global effort:

- A set of coordinated transparency reforms has made beneficial ownership and financial-account information far harder to hide; several hundred billion dollars of previously opaque wealth are now visible to tax authorities.
- An enhanced global minimum tax is broadly in place for big firms, blunting profit-shifting and raising tens of billions in extra revenue each year for low- and middle-income countries (allocated via formula and technical assistance).
- A functional debt-restructuring panel has resolved multiple sovereign cases more quickly,

freeing fiscal space for schools and climate-resilient infrastructure.

- The Green Climate Fund and a dedicated loss & damage facility are replenished with grant finance, enabling coastal and island nations to invest in relocation, protective works, and disaster recovery without borrowing.

- Trade rules have been recalibrated to permit technology transfer for key green sectors, and regional manufacturing clusters have grown on the back of preferential procurement and development finance.

- Domestic politics have shifted: citizens in richer countries see their taxes help public goods internationally and spot fewer headlines about billionaires' offshore tricks; small businesses in developing countries compete more fairly.

These are practical rather than utopian steps. They require leadership, persistence, and credible enforcement. But they are implementable. The real obstacle is political will.

10. A Short Political Playbook: How to Move Fast Without Breaking Things

A feasible political strategy maps domestic wins to international demands.

1. **Domestic transparency wins first.** Build public

mandates for beneficial-ownership disclosure and country-by-country reporting at home. These create legitimacy for demanding reciprocal action internationally.

2. **Bilateral and plurilateral coalitions.** Like-minded countries (a coalition of the willing) can create standards that others join. The EU's approach to gatekeeper regulation and tax transparency shows plurilateral action scales.
3. **Use international institutions instrumentally.** Push for reforms in the OECD, IMF, and UN while using regional blocs to pressure laggards.
4. **Link climate finance to tax and debt reform.** Show developed-country electorates that tackling their own tax abuse frees funds to meet climate obligations and mitigates migration pressures in the medium term.
5. **Tell human stories.** Connect abstract reforms to stories — a clinic that can open, a school that can hire teachers — so publics understand the stakes.

11. Solidarity as Strategy — The Moral and Material Case

Global redistribution is both moral and strategic. It is moral because the least-responsible and least-resourced nations face the worst harms from a crisis they did not cause; it is strategic because global instability — from unresolved debt crises, climate-driven displacement, or pandemics — rebounds quickly into wealthy countries' economies and politics.

The architecture of global piñata economics is stubborn because it benefits powerful actors who have incentives to preserve it. But history shows structures that look immovable can change. Multilateralism has retooled itself when public pressure, technical innovation, and political leadership converge. Reducing secrecy, reforming tax rules, creating a faster debt-restructuring process, and scaling grant-based climate finance are not metaphysical impossibilities — they are policy choices. They require sustained coalition building: among countries, across political movements, and with those private actors who profit from fairer rules.

If you want candy flowing to where it's needed — to resilient infrastructure, to education, to adaptation and reconstruction — then you must think like an international designer: build rules that travel with capital, make evasion more costly than compliance, and embed solidarity into institutional architecture. Domestic reforms matter. But the big levers — tax cooperation, debt workouts, climate transfers, and fair trade rules — are international. Global solidarity is not charity; it is a rational design for a stable world in which the piñata's candy is shared in a way that keeps the party going for everyone.

A Shared Celebration: The Vision of a Redistributed Society

Imagine, for a moment, walking into a town square on a bright Saturday. The market is lively: a mix of stalls run by co-ops and small businesses, a municipal bakery selling breads at modest prices, a corner clinic offering walk-in care with a sign that reads "Everyone Welcome," and a community center advertising free early-childhood programs and evening adult classes. Children splash in a public fountain while their parents sit under an awning having coffee paid for by a public cup scheme. Transit arrives on time. People you meet smile in the way of neighbors who trust one another. Above the square a banner announces a civic festival celebrating local art, with the words: "Shared Prosperity, Shared Pride."

That tableau is not a pie-in-the-sky utopia. It's a picture of what a society looks like when the rules that shape opportunity and access are redesigned to favor circulation, dignity, and shared investment. It is a society in which collective institutions do the heavy lifting so that daily life is easier, more creative, and more secure. It is a society with universal healthcare that treats care as a right, education that opens doors rather than closes them, dignified work that fosters community rather than atomized precariousness, public goods that sustain civic life, and democratic institutions that actually answer to broad, not narrow, publics.

This chapter paints that vision in detail. It is both inspirational and practical—anchored in what we already know works, and honest about trade-offs and political work required. I'll show what tangible changes would feel like in everyday life, summarize the evidence that public investment pays off, and explain the cultural shifts that turn policy into lived reality. The goal is not to sell perfection but to make a clear case: redistribution is not just about cutting the slices differently; it is about redesigning the table so the feast is bigger and everyone gets a plate.

1. Universal Healthcare: Health as a Public Good, Not a Market Gamble

Picture waking up sick and knowing you will see a clinician that day without three bills later and without fear of losing your home to medical debt. That is the basic human security of universal healthcare.

What the system looks like

In a redistributed society, healthcare is organized around universality, prevention, and cost-effective delivery. Primary care is widely available and free at point of use. Mental health and preventive services are emphasized alongside acute care. Prescription drugs are priced comparatively low because public negotiations and reference pricing systems keep costs down. Long-term care—often a neglected area—is funded and regulated so that aging does not mean financial ruin.

Hospital networks are integrated with community clinics, social services, and housing supports so clinicians can treat the whole person. Electronic health records are interoperable and patient-controlled. Importantly, healthcare financing is progressive and sustainable: a combination of contributed revenue (progressive taxation) and efficient public administration that eliminates wasteful overhead in fragmented billing systems.

Why it matters

Universal healthcare reduces mortality, improves productivity, and reduces inequality. Healthy people are better able to work, learn, and participate civically. Removing the insecurity of medical debt also reduces the precarity that pushes families into poverty. Public systems are better at negotiating prices, standardizing quality, and investing in population health measures (vaccination, screening, harm reduction).

Evidence and outcomes

Countries that organize healthcare as a public good tend to have better population health metrics and lower per-person spending on health care. Systems that emphasize primary care and prevention lower hospitalizations and chronic disease burdens. The returns are moral and economic: fewer catastrophic financial events, more consistent labor participation, and lower public spending on emergency social services.

2. Universal Education: From Early Childhood to Lifelong Learning

Education is often described as the great equalizer. But to do that work it must be universal, well-resourced, and connected to opportunity.

What the system looks like

A redistributed education system begins before kindergarten. Free, high-quality early childhood education is available to every family; it is staffed by well-trained professionals and integrated with pediatric and social services. K–12 schooling is financed equitably so a child's address does not determine the quality of their classroom or the resources available for music, science labs, or counseling. Schools are community hubs that offer after-school programs, language services, and family supports.

Higher education is affordable and diverse in pathways. Public universities and technical institutes offer low- or no-tuition options, apprenticeships are scaled and connected to living-wage caps, and lifelong learning accounts help adults re-skilled without plunging into debt. Credentialing systems are broadened to value demonstrated skill and experience as much as degrees—portable certifications, apprenticeships, and employer-neutral assessments expand access to good jobs.

Why it matters

Education at all stages amplifies human capability, reduces intergenerational inequality, and fuels innovation. Early childhood investment has among the highest social returns of any public program—children who receive quality care are more likely to graduate, earn more, and have better health outcomes. Equitable K–12 funding narrows the achievement gap and increases economic mobility. Affordable postsecondary options prevent debt traps that otherwise hoard opportunity.

Evidence and outcomes

Classic longitudinal studies and contemporary policy reviews consistently show large returns on early childhood investment—both in terms of earnings and societal benefits like reduced crime and improved health. When school funding is de-linked from local property taxes and pooled, disparities in facilities, teacher quality, and extracurriculars shrink quickly. Countries and regions that expanded vocational pathways along with university options show better alignment between training and labor-market demand, and lower youth unemployment.

3. Dignified Work: Living Wages, Voice, and Safe Conditions

The future of work needn't be precarious. Dignified work is built on three pillars: fair pay, worker voice, and safety nets that recognize the nonlinear nature of modern careers.

What dignified work looks like

A dignified labor system guarantees a living wage floor indexed to local costs, encourages collective bargaining (sectoral where appropriate), and extends portable benefits to nonstandard workers. Gig platforms and subcontracting firms are regulated to ensure transparency of algorithms, rights to redress, and individuals' ability to organize. Paid family and sick leave, universal childcare, and unemployment insurance with retraining supports make transitions manageable.

Worker voice is institutionalized: works councils, co-determination on corporate boards in some sectors, and legal frameworks that protect organizing rights create a structural balance between labor and capital. Health and safety inspections are robust; whistleblower protections are enforced; automation is guided by social bargains that protect employment and re-skilling pathways rather than simply replacing jobs with layoffs.

Why it matters

Work is not only income; it is identity and social participation. When jobs pay enough and offer predictable schedules, families thrive; communities are more stable; civic participation increases. Worker voice improves firm decision-making—evidence suggests workplaces with stronger employee representation are more productive and better at long-term planning.

Evidence and outcomes

Minimum-wage studies show modest increases lacking large employment losses in well-designed policy settings; sectoral bargaining has compressed wage gaps in many developed economies; countries with strong worker representation enjoy higher productivity and lower inequality. Portable benefits (retirement, health savings) reduce the precarity associated with gig work and turn economic shocks into manageable transitions rather than poverty traps.

4. Thriving Public Commons: Parks, Transit, Libraries, and Civic Culture

Public goods are the scaffolding of civic life. A redistributed society invests in commons that are accessible, well-maintained, and culturally rich.

What the commons look like

Public transit is frequent, affordable, and clean; it connects neighborhoods rather than bifurcating them. Parks and green spaces proliferate in dense urban centers and are maintained equitably. Libraries are reinvented as civic tech hubs offering free internet access, training, and community programming. Public broadcasting and arts funding ensure that cultural life is robust, diverse, and not reduced to market logics.

Municipal services—waste, water, broadband—are treated as essential infrastructure with universal access obligations. Community land trusts and permanently affordable housing tools maintain mixed-income neighborhoods. Public spaces host festivals, markets, and civic forums; they are places where people can meet, deliberate, and relax without a price tag.

Why it matters

Commons reduce the individual cost of living, create shared experiences that foster trust, and underpin economic activity. Effective transit expands labor markets; parks reduce heat islands and improve public health; libraries and community centers increase digital inclusion and social cohesion. Public procurement that prioritizes local suppliers and co-ops keeps wealth circulating in communities.

Evidence and outcomes

Investments in transit reduce commute times and widen job matching; green space correlates with better health outcomes and child development; broadband access increases participation in digital economies. Public cultural funding has multiplier effects: it creates jobs, supports small businesses, and enhances tourism.

5. Stronger Democracy: Participation, Transparency, and Accountability

Redistribution depends crucially on democratic institutions resilient to capture and responsive to citizens. A redistributed society reforms the rules so democracy works for everyone—not just the well-connected.

What stronger democracy looks like

Campaign finance limits and public matching amplify small donors and reduce the sway of concentrated money. Disclosure regimes for lobbying and beneficial ownership make influence transparent. Participatory budgeting, citizens' assemblies, and devolved governance create real channels for community input into public spending. Administrative independence for regulators and a robust, well-funded public civil service ensure consistent policy implementation.

Legal protections for protest and media pluralism safeguard civic space. Judicial appointment processes are insulated from partisan capture, and citizen oversight bodies audit public programs to keep them accountable. Digital platforms are regulated to prevent manipulation and ensure public debate is not dominated by paid amplification.

Why it matters

When citizens can see who funds policy and can meaningfully participate, legitimacy increases and policymaking aligns better with public needs. Transparency reduces corruption; participatory processes generate better policy by drawing on local knowledge and creating constituency support for public goods.

Evidence and outcomes

Countries with stronger transparency norms and public financing show lower corruption indices, higher public trust, and more durable public investments. Participatory budgeting experiments demonstrate improved targeting of municipal spending and increased civic engagement. When institutions are designed to be responsive, citizens are more likely to support redistributive policies.

6. Cultural Shifts: From Hoarding to Stewardship

Policy alone is not enough. The deepest transformation is cultural. A redistributed society cultivates values—stewardship, reciprocity, and civic pride—that change how people think about wealth, status, and the common good.

What cultural change looks like

- **Status is reframed.** Prestige attaches not only to accumulation but to contribution—teachers, nurses, public managers, and community leaders are valued. Wealth becomes less of a moral token and more of a set of social responsibilities.

- **Philanthropy is reimagined.** Instead of operating as a substitute for public funding, philanthropy complements public effort in transparent partnerships; foundations are accountable and must work within democratic priorities.

- **Consumption norms shift.** Social signaling moves away from conspicuous consumption to communal consumption—shared gardens, public festivals, and locally produced goods.

- **Education in civic virtues.** Schools teach civic literacy alongside technical skills—how budgets are made, how to participate, how to form associations.

These cultural changes are subtle and cumulative. Narratives about success emphasize fair opportunity and social contribution rather than purely individual triumph. The meritocratic story is recast: effort matters, but so does the social condition that makes effort meaningful.

Why it matters

Norms shape politics. If people celebrate hoarding and see redistribution as moral punishment, deep reforms are impossible. When cultural values prize mutual aid and public investment, democratic coalitions are more durable and policy can be ambitious without constant backsliding.

7. Evidence That Public Investment Pays Off: Return on Public Goods

A redistributed society is not about taking away for the sake of equality; it's an investment strategy that increases the size and quality of what's produced. Here are key evidence-backed domains where public investment yields outsized returns.

Early childhood education

Investment in high-quality early childhood programs produces large long-term returns through higher earnings, reduced criminality, better health, and improved educational attainment. Economists who study this field have found that the social rates of return are often high—every dollar invested can yield multiple dollars in societal benefit across decades.

Universal healthcare

Systems that prioritize primary care and prevention reduce downstream costs. Preventive care and early treatment lower chronic disease prevalence, reduce emergency room use, and keep labor participation higher. Negotiated drug prices and streamlined administration cut waste. The net effect is better health at lower or comparable per-capita spending.

Infrastructure and transit

Investments in transit and physical infrastructure boost productivity by reducing travel times, enabling labor mobility, and connecting firms to labor pools. Infrastructure investment also has multiplier effects on employment and local business formation. Modern resilient infrastructure reduces future disaster costs and enables green transitions.

Education and training

Higher levels of public education investment correlate with greater human capital, higher GDP per capita, and more resilient societies. Vocational training that matches industry needs reduces structural unemployment and smooths technological transitions.

Social insurance and resilience

Social insurance programs (unemployment insurance, pensions, disability) stabilize demand during downturns, prevent severe poverty, and allow for smoother economic cycles. These programs act as automatic stabilizers, reducing the depth of recessions and facilitating faster recoveries.

8. Equity and Growth: Not a Zero-Sum Game

A common critique is that redistribution slows growth. The evidence suggests a more nuanced reality: well-designed redistribution that funds public goods and builds human capital is growth-enhancing.

Mechanisms for pro-growth redistribution

- **Demand stimulus.** Putting more purchasing power in the hands of lower- and middle-income individuals increases consumption and therefore demand for goods and services produced locally.

- **Human capital formation.** Public investment in health and education raises productivity, innovation, and the capacity for technological adoption.

- **Reduced misallocation.** When essential services are widely available, talent can be deployed where it is most productive rather than trapped in survival strategies.

- **Stability and trust.** Redistribution that reduces extreme inequality stabilizes democracy, lowers the risk of destabilizing shocks, and creates regulatory regimes conducive to long-term investment.

Examples across advanced economies show that moderate redistribution coexists with strong productivity and innovation. Scandinavian countries, for instance, combine productive markets with deep social supports; they are not growthless utopias but dynamic economies with high living standards and strong social cohesion.

9. Justice and Dignity: Beyond Numbers

Redistribution is not only economic engineering; it is about dignity. A society that guarantees healthcare, education, housing, and decent work affirms a basic moral claim: membership in a polity conveys rights, not debts.

Dignity changes how people view one another. When safety nets exist, relationships are less transactional and more communal. People are freer to pursue meaningful work, creative projects, caregiving, and civic engagement because they are not always in survival mode. That freedom—hard to quantify—is one of the central justifications for redistributive policies.

10. Getting There: The Political and Cultural Work Ahead

The vision sketched above is aspirational but grounded in policy realism. The political path to get there blends immediate tangible wins (wage increases, childcare slots, procurement reforms) with institution-building (tax enforcement, labor law modernization, campaign finance reform) and cultural narratives that reshape how we value the common good.

Movements, civic coalitions, responsive political leadership, and enlightened business practices all have to converge. The practical steps are many: local pilots that demonstrate feasibility, legal defense structures to protect reforms, strategic sequencing to prevent evasion, and international coordination where cross-border issues matter.

Most of all, persistence matters. The institutions of redistribution are not one-off laws but durable systems that must be defended, funded, and iterated. That requires both short-term wins to build momentum and long-term investments to lock in change.

11. A Day in the Life: Lived Experience in a Redistributed Society

To make this concrete, imagine a day in the life of Mara, a single parent in a mid-sized city that has embraced the principles in this chapter.

She wakes to a public transit app that tells her the bus is three minutes away. A subsidized childcare center staffed with trained early-childhood educators opens at 7 a.m., and she drops her seven-year-old off for breakfast and a play-based curriculum. Her clinic visit for a chronic condition is scheduled for that afternoon at a community health center, and the nurse coordinator calls to remind her about a subsidized medication program. Her employer, a mid-sized cooperative, pays a living wage and offers profit-sharing; the company is able to offer that because procurement rules favor responsible employers and because local demand has increased with higher wages.

In the evening Mara enrolls in an evening vocational course supported by a city training fund. Her neighbor, who used to work in precarious app-based gig work, now co-owns a platform cooperative that provides delivery services in the neighborhood. On Saturday, the family goes to the public library not only for books but for a community concert in the park where a municipal arts grant funded local performers. Mara participates in a participatory budgeting meeting where residents vote on small infrastructure projects and a new after-school program.

This is not a fantasy of plenty; it's a rebalancing that turns private insecurity into shared possibility. The difference is that the structures around Mara—healthcare, childcare, work, learning, and civic life—are designed to make ordinary choices easier and dignified.

12. Risks and Trade-Offs: Honest Challenges

No vision is risk-free. There are trade-offs to deliberate redistribution:

- **Fiscal constraints and priorities.** Public budgets are finite. The political challenge is choosing investments with the highest social returns and resisting regressions that cut key programs for short-term political gain.

- **Administration and corruption risks.** Programs require strong institutions to implement equitably; weak governance can misallocate resources. Transparency, independent audits, and civic oversight reduce those risks.

- **International pressures.** Global capital seeks escape routes; hence the need for domestic-international sequencing and cooperation to prevent flight and arbitrage.

- **Cultural resistance.** Changing norms takes time—campaigns, storytelling, and civic education matter.

Recognizing these risks makes the project more credible, not less. Good policy designs include safeguards, evaluation mechanisms, and conditionalities that preserve program integrity without undermining dignity.

13. How Success Looks: Benchmarks to Aim For

A redistributed society can be tracked with clear benchmarks:

- **Economic security.** Reduced rate of catastrophic health expenses, lower poverty rates, and a marked decline in households one emergency away from destitution.

- **Labor market quality.** Higher median wages, rising share of income going to labor, lower income volatility, higher union coverage or representation rates.

- **Educational outcomes.** Narrower achievement gaps by socioeconomic status; higher postsecondary attainment across demographics.

- **Public goods access.** Increased transit ridership, higher broadband coverage, and more public green space per capita.

- **Democratic health.** Higher turnout, lower measures of corruption, and broader public approval of institutions.

- **Civic trust and cultural indicators.** Surveys showing increased trust in neighbors and institutions, a shift in attitudes about redistribution and civic responsibility.

These are measurable and policy-relevant metrics that allow course correction and accountability.

14. Final Case for the Party: Why Redistribution Is Worth It

There is a moral argument for redistribution that is simple: a society that can feed, heal, educate, and protect all its members chooses justice over neglect. There is also an economic argument: public investment tends to pay for itself in higher productivity, lower social costs, and more stable growth. Finally, there is a political argument: equality fosters legitimacy and lowers the risk of destabilizing conflicts.

The redistributed society I describe is neither tidy nor effortless. It requires bargaining, fiscal choices, international cooperation, and cultural work. But it also creates public conditions in which people can flourish, where risk is beared collectively rather than catastrophically, and where the capacity for collective action grows.

This is the party we want to throw: one where everyone gets a plate and the music is for us all.

From Vision to Practice

You have read earlier chapters about the tools—the sticks, the legal strategies, the international reforms, and the political countermeasures. This chapter shows what those tools are for. The final bend of the book is about the work of building coalitions, telling a new story about success and obligation, and organizing durable institutions that outlast electoral cycles.

Start small. Win a childcare expansion here, a procurement reform there, a living-wage ordinance, a transparency registry. Use these wins to build public pressure for bigger changes: progressive taxes, healthcare expansion, international cooperation on tax and climate finance. Anchor policy in evidence, defend it with strong institutions, and sustain it with cultural change.

The redistributive society is not a single law or a single leader's vision. It is a long, patient project of designing institutions that respect dignity and spread power. It is a shared celebration—one we organize and protect together. Let the music start. Grab the stick, swing with care and strategy, and pass the candy freely. The party is better that way.

Roadmap & Mobilization — How We Win

This is the bootcamp, the campaign manual, and the pep talk rolled into one. All the diagnosis, the tools, the counterplay and the vision in the earlier chapters come down to this: people power. Redistribution isn't a policy spreadsheet; it's a sustained political project. It is built by organizers, unions, voters, storytellers, lawyers, journalists, cities, and international allies working in concert. This chapter is a practical movement playbook — a blueprint for how to move from ideas to durable gains.

I'll walk through concrete, tactical sequences: grassroots organizing and base-building; union strategies that scale power; electoral work that changes who gets to write the rules; narrative campaigns that reshape public feeling; legal playbooks that defend and expand space for action; international networks that amplify pressure and constrain capital flight; metrics and monitoring to know if you're winning; and institutional safeguards to make wins sticky (constitutional protections, anti-capture measures, procurement rules). I end with a rousing call to collective action — because structure and will both matter.

Throughout, this chapter aims to be pragmatic. It recognizes trade-offs and the adaptive power of opposition. It assumes the piñata's defenders will fight back. So each tactic includes preemption and defense: legal defense funds for SLAPPs, narrative pre-bunking for PR attacks, data transparency to blunt secrecy. This is the playbook for a long campaign — not a one-off protest. Let's go.

1. Grassroots Organizing: Building a Durable Base

Organizing is the heart of power. Policies can be drafted and courts can rule, but without a base to pressure politicians, implementers, and corporations, reforms will be fragile. Grassroots organizing is about long-term relational work: recruiting, training, mobilizing, and sustaining people across neighborhoods and workplaces.

Core principles

- **Start with relationships, not messages.** Deep canvassing, one-on-one conversations, listening sessions, and house meetings create durable commitment. Relationship-driven organizing (the Ganz model and variants) produces people who will act when called.

- **Organize places, not issues.** Build power around institutions (neighborhood associations, schools, churches, tenant unions). Place-based networks make turnout and sustained pressure easier.

- **Move from service to power.** Direct service (legal clinics, food distribution) can be an entry point; translate that into organizing by linking individual needs to systemic causes.

- **Train leaders.** Invest in leadership pipelines from the base so organizers are not the only ones who can lead actions or speak publicly. Rotate responsibilities; cultivate local champions.

Tactics and tools

- **Canvassing & relational outreach.** Use a "three-visit" strategy: listen, invite, and recruit. Relational organizing is more predictive of action than mass media appeals.

- **House meetings and neighborhood assemblies.** Small gatherings convert sympathy into commitment. They are where people practice telling their story — powerful in narrative campaigns later.

- **Digital organizing to scale, but not replace.** Use texting, social media, and CRMs (e.g., NationBuilder, VAN) to coordinate, but always tie online work to offline relational touchpoints.

- **Volunteer management & retention.** Create clear volunteer pathways, celebrate small wins, and avoid burnout with rotating responsibilities and realistic expectations.

- **Mutual aid as organizing infrastructure.** Build reciprocity: mutual-aid projects develop skills, trust, and cross-class alliances.

Metrics for grassroots power

- Number of active organizers and trained leaders by neighborhood.

- Contact and conversion rates (how many first conversations lead to commitments to volunteer or attend).

- Turnout rates among contacted households vs. baseline.

- Sustained action rates (how many volunteers remain active after 6 and 12 months).

2. Union Strategy: Rebuilding Labor Power for the 21st Century

A strong labor movement is the single most effective machine for durable redistribution. Unions raise wages, normalize benefits, and make employer accountability systemic. The current moment — with young workers energizing drives and high public support for unions — is an opening.

Strategic pillars

- **Organize where workers are: new sectors and tech-enabled work.** Move beyond legacy sectors into gig, service, care, and tech-adjacent industries. Use tactics like "salting" (organizers joining workplaces to organize from within) and cross-site campaigns to scale leverage.

- **Sectoral and pattern bargaining.** Seek bargaining at the industry level where possible (sectoral bargaining), which avoids firm-by-firm fragmentation and sets minimum standards across entire supply chains.

- **Hybrid models: staff unions + rank-and-file militancy.** Professionalize campaign support while amplifying worker-led initiatives to maintain credibility and momentum.

- **Strategic strikes and leverage actions.** Use targeted strikes, slowdowns, public demonstrations and boycotts timed to pressure points (peak seasons, contract deadlines, shareholder meetings). Cross-sector solidarity actions multiply impact.

Tactics and innovations

- **Salting and targeted internal organizing.** Train organizers to enter workplaces strategically and build internal networks; focus on converting insiders into leaders.

- **Community-labor alliances.** Link labor fights to community concerns (affordable housing, transit) to broaden support and reduce employer leverage.

- **Legal readiness.** Anticipate union-busting with rapid-response legal teams, pro-bono networks, and public campaigns exposing unfair labor practices.

- **Use bargaining to win broader standards.** Secure clauses that improve subcontractor practices, require living wages in procurement contracts, and include training funds for workers.

Metrics for union power

- Union density rates and bargaining coverage (share of workers covered by a collective agreement).
- Win rate for organizing campaigns and average time-to-win.
- Wage gains negotiated versus local median wage growth.
- Spillover effects (wage floor changes in nonunion firms in the same sector).

3. Electoral Work: Changing the Rules Through Elections

Elections decide policy windows. The goal is not only electing allies but altering the incentives that shape institutional behavior — through candidate recruitment, voter mobilization, and building durable electoral infrastructure.

Strategy: think long-term

- **Prepare 3–5 electoral cycles.** Build a bench of leaders; support local races that build long-term governing credibility (school boards, city councils, county supervisors). Local offices matter for procurement, zoning, and education funding.

- **Candidate recruitment & training.** Support community leaders to run with training on messaging, fundraising, and governing. Candidates who are organizers understand coalition-building and governance trade-offs.

- **Voter mobilization & protection.** Combine relational canvassing with voter-protection teams (poll monitors, legal hotlines, rapid-response) to maximize turnout in key precincts.

- **Policy-first campaigns.** Run on concrete, tangible promises (childcare slots, living wage ordinance, municipal broadband) that test governance capacity and build credibility.

Electoral infrastructure

- **Small-donor networks and match programs.** Develop fundraising architectures that rely on small contributions and public matching where possible; reduce dependence on big donors.

- **Data capacity.** Invest in databases, field modeling, and analysis to target turnout effectively.

- **Campaign-labor-community partnerships.** Use union and community networks to mobilize simultaneously in targeted precincts.

Safeguards & anti-capture

- **Campaign-finance reform as both policy and practice.** Advocate for public financing that makes running affordable, paired with disclosure rules to reduce dark-money influence.

- **Ethics and revolving-door rules.** Push for rules that limit lobbyist-candidate ties and require disclosure of outside income and gifts.

Metrics for electoral impact

- Voter registration and turnout improvements in target precincts.

- Number of organizer-candidates trained and elected.

- Policy wins by elected allies within first two years.

- Reduction in outside money in targeted races.

4. Narrative Campaigns: Winning the Frame

Power without a story is fragile. Narrative campaigns create public permission for change. They make the moral case simple and connect thesis to daily life.

Principles of effective narrative work

- **Diagnose, prognose, and motivate.** A strong frame identifies the problem (diagnosis), offers a realistic solution path (prognosis), and calls people to action (motivation). Academic work on framing shows these three elements are essential.

- **Use values-first language.** Lead with core values (security, dignity, fairness, reciprocity) and then give policy details. Stories of people affected by the problem humanize abstract policy.

- **Test, iterate, and localize.** Message testing (A/B testing, focus groups) finds what resonates locally; tailor frames to local concerns and cultural norms.

Tactics and tools

- **Narrative maps.** Build simple materials: one-sentence frames, 30-second personal stories, and 500-word explainers for journalists.

- **Rapid-response media teams.** Train spokespeople, prepare op-eds, and deploy rapid rebuttals to misinformation.

- **Cultural connects.** Partner with artists, faith leaders, and local influencers to spread frames beyond political audiences.

- **Pre-bunking.** Anticipate common scare frames (jobs lost, taxes skyrocketing) and test counters that preempt those messages before opponents run them.

Metrics for narrative success

- Message uptake in media (mentions of frame in local/national reporting).
- Polling shifts on support for specific policies post-campaign.
- Social-media engagement and sentiment measures.
- Persuasion effect measurements from experiments or targeted polling.

5. Legal Tactics: Litigation, Defense Funds, and the Anti-SLAPP Arsenal

Lawsuits will come. Opponents weaponize courts to delay and intimidate. Legal readiness is essential.

Defensive measures

- **Legal defense funds.** Pool resources for bail, litigation, and representation — essential for protecting organizers, journalists, and NGOs targeted with SLAPPs or injunctions. Many movements have built dedicated funds to absorb legal attrition.
- **Anti-SLAPP advocacy.** Push for strong anti-SLAPP statutes that allow quick dismissal of vexatious suits and recovery of legal fees for

defendants. Where legislative reform is slow, prepare rapid-response legal strategies and public exposure to make lawsuits reputationally costly to plaintiffs.

- **Strategic litigation.** Use offensive litigation to create protections (e.g., labor-rights rulings, voting rights, administrative law cases). Identify cases with strong facts that could set favorable precedents.

Rapid-response legal operations

- **Pro bono networks and partnerships.** Cultivate relationships with law firms and legal clinics able to mobilize quickly.

- **Document preservation & FOIA readiness.** Train staff to preserve evidence and use disclosure laws to pull documents that embarrass opponents or reveal capture.

- **Court of public opinion.** Legal fights work better with parallel media strategies exposing nuisance litigation motives.

Metrics for legal readiness

- Time to mobilize counsel after a legal threat.

- Funds available in legal defense pool relative to projected needs.

- Number of successful anti-SLAPP defenses or dismissals.

6. International Networks: Transnational Solidarity and Pressure

Many targets are global: multinational corporations, tax havens, and supply chains. International networks multiply leverage — sharing tactics, coordinating pressure, and constraining regulatory arbitrage.

Networks and tools

- **Transnational advocacy networks.** Link local NGOs to international NGOs, unions, and investigative journalists to amplify cases across jurisdictions. Keck & Sikkink's model shows how naming-and-shaming across borders can change behaviors.

- **Cross-border action windows.** Coordinate synchronized actions (boycotts, shareholder campaigns, protests) timed to global shareholders' meetings or regulatory deadlines.

- **Shared research & data platforms.** Pool investigative resources (beneficial ownership, supply chain data) to expose opaque structures and inform policy proposals.

- **International legal strategies.** Use human-rights mechanisms, multilateral complaint mechanisms, and coordinated litigation to create pressure points.

Institutional allies

- **Engage sympathetic states and multilateral institutions** for policy leverage (e.g., for anti-tax-haven rules, debt relief, labor standards).

- **Form regional blocs** to carry collective bargaining power (e.g., municipalities sharing procurement rules, union internationals coordinating industrial action).

Metrics for international leverage

- Number of cross-border coalitions built and active.

- Volume and reach of international media coverage of targeted issues.

- Policy changes or enforcement actions coordinated across jurisdictions.

7. Metrics for Movement Success: What to Measure and Why

You can't manage what you don't measure. Movement metrics are both tactical (did actions produce immediate leverage?)

and strategic (are we shifting power over time?). Use mixed metrics: input, process, output, outcome, and impact.

Suggested dashboard

- **Power-building metrics:** active organizers, local chapters, volunteer retention, leader training completion rates. (Process)
- **Mobilization metrics:** turnout for actions, petition signatures, meeting attendance, number of trained spokespeople. (Output)
- **Policy impact metrics:** number of ordinances passed, administrative policy changes, court victories, procurement contracts altered. (Outcome)
- **Structural metrics:** union density, bargaining coverage, percentage of top marginal income taxed, share of public procurement to local/co-op firms. (Impact)
- **Narrative & public opinion metrics:** polling shifts on key frames, media mentions, social sentiment. (Outcome)
- **Resilience metrics:** legal defense fund adequacy, number of successful defenses against SLAPPs, staff turnover and burnout indicators.

Frameworks like the "Power of Social Movements" help operationalize metrics for how movements build power. Use mixed quantitative and qualitative indicators — personal stories and case studies matter for persuasion as much as numbers.

8. Safeguards to Institutionalize Gains: Make It Hard to Roll Back

Winning reforms is only half the battle. Make wins durable by embedding legal and institutional protections that raise the cost of rollback.

Structural protections

- **Constitutional or statutory anchors.** Where possible, anchor core rights (voting, labor rights, basic healthcare) in robust legal frameworks that require supermajorities to dismantle. This is context-dependent but powerful where feasible.

- **Anti-capture measures.** Strengthen disclosure laws, cooling-off periods for regulators-turned-lobbyists, and conflict-of-interest rules to reduce the chance of regulatory capture.

- **Independent agencies with protected budgets.** Fund and insulate enforcement bodies (labor boards, tax authorities, competition authorities) from political and financial pressure; consider multi-year funding guarantees and public reporting requirements.

- **Procurement and budgetary locks.** Use procurement rules and dedicated funding streams (e.g., trust funds for childcare) to ensure program continuity beyond electoral cycles.

- **Sunset review with automatic renewal thresholds.** If sunset clauses are politically necessary, tie renewal to transparent performance metrics that make rollbacks politically costly if public benefit is evident.

Civic and legal anchors

- **Public-interest litigation capacity.** Build institutions that can defend progressive regulations and challenge rollbacks.

- **Participatory governance.** Institutionalize participatory budgeting, citizens' assemblies, and oversight bodies to keep officials accountable and build civic ownership.

- **Media and transparency safeguards.** Protect investigative journalism with shield laws, public-interest grants, and anti-SLAPP protections so rollbacks cannot be hidden.

9. Sequencing & Phasing: From Local Wins to National Lock-In

Tactical sequencing matters. Here's a tested path that minimizes adaptation by opponents and builds durable power:

1. **Transparency & enforcement readiness.** Fix disclosure so future revenue and enforcement have teeth. Transparency builds political legitimacy for taxing and spending reforms.
2. **Local wins & pilots.** Municipal living-wage laws, procurement reforms, public childcare pilots, and municipal broadband demonstrate feasibility and build constituencies.
3. **Labor & competition moves.** Strengthen organizing rights and local anti-monopoly actions to re-balance power before national-level tax changes.
4. **Tax-base fixes & progressive rates.** With enforcement in place and public trust built, close loopholes and raise marginal rates, dedicating funds to programs with visible returns.
5. **Institutionalization.** Pass legal protections, secure budgets for enforcement, and embed participatory structures to make rollbacks harder.
6. **Scale internationally.** Coordinate cross-border measures (tax transparency, procurement harmonization, international labor standards) to prevent capital flight and arbitrate gaps.

Each phase builds the political capital necessary for the next. Local wins not only help people now; they provide proof that reforms work and build defenders.

10. Defense & Counterattack: Expect Pushback — Plan for It

Resistance will come. Prepare for five arenas of counterattack — PR/propaganda, legal harassment, lobbying, economic pressure, and repression — and preempt each.

- **PR & narrative attacks:** Build rapid-response media teams, use pre-bunking, and show human stories of benefits to blunt scare tactics.

- **Legal harassment (SLAPPs & injunctions):** Fund legal defense pools and push anti-SLAPP laws; publicize abusive suits to turn public ire against plaintiffs.

- **Lobbying & capture:** Use transparency registries, naming-and-shaming, and public pressure to constrain lobbying; promote ethics reforms.

- **Economic pressure:** Opponents may threaten divestment or relocation. Counter with local procurement, incentives for responsible firms, and narrative pressure on reputationally exposed actors.

- **Repression:** Protect protesters with legal aid, rapid-response medics, and digital security; internationalize repression stories to create political costs.

Defensive planning is not defensive pessimism — it's realistic strategy.

11. Movement Financing & Sustainability

Sustained campaigns need money that preserves independence.

- **Hybrid financing:** Combine small-donor fundraising, foundation grants, earned income (training, consulting), and membership dues to avoid domination by any one funder.

- **Legal funds & bail funds:** Maintain dedicated reserves for litigation and arrests.

- **Staffing & burnout prevention:** Budget for staff wages that are livable; rotate responsibilities and invest in mental-health supports for organizers.

12. A Final Tactical Checklist

Before you step into the field, run through this short checklist:

- Have you mapped power — who benefits, who loses, who can be a swing constituency?

- Do you have a relational base and a tested narrative?

- Is your legal defense plan funded and ready?

- Are your metrics set up to measure power and outcomes?

- Have you built cross-sector alliances (labor, small business, parents, tenants)?

- Is enforcement capacity in place or funded?
- Do you have an international plan for the cross-border aspects of your target?
- Are procurement, budget, and institutional safeguards ready to lock in wins?

If you can answer yes to most of these, you're ready to act. If not, prioritize building the missing pieces.

13. A Rousing Call: The Political Imagination Meets the Long Game

You have the tools. You have the stories. You have history on your side: change rarely arrives from a single speech or a single election. It accumulates — from kitchen-table conversations, seed budgets in municipal councils, union halls where workers find their voice, courtroom victories that set precedents, and international pressure that closes secrecy holes. The piñata's fortifications are human-made and therefore human-changeable.

This is a long campaign, and the work is often granular. Celebrate small wins. Make time for rest and community. Protect your people and your institutions. Build for the next generation of leaders. Tell stories so powerful they become the way people explain their lives.

Organize like your neighbor's future depends on it — because it does. Bargain like your children's schools depend on it — because they do. Vote like your rights hang in the balance —

because often they do. Join like your strength depends on solidarity — because it always has.

We win not because we are smarter than those who hoard, but because we are more numerous when we are organized, more credible when we govern locally, and more persistent when we care for our people. Start with one neighborhood, one workplace, one city. Build in ways that scale. Use the sticks in earlier chapters, but remember the most powerful stick: people who refuse to accept the story that scarcity is natural and who insist on a different future.

Grab the stick. Call your neighbor. Train a leader. File the brief. Run the ad. March to the council. Vote in the fall. Build institutions that protect the gains. Pass the candy.

The road is long, but the destination is worth it. We're not just changing policy; we're changing the story we tell our children about what a fair and flourishing society looks like. Get to work — together.

About the Author

Lucas Brooks makes complex economic systems readable. With a background in political economy and years of experience advising community campaigns, he brings clarity and urgency to the fight against inequality.